HISTORY of Economic Theory

VOLUME 1

Presented by
Coventry House Publishing

ISBN: 0615817890
ISBN-13: 978-0615817897

CONTENTS

An Investigation of the Cause
of the Present High Price of Provisions

T.R. Malthus; 1800

Among the many causes that have been assigned of the present high price of provisions, I am much inclined to suspect, that the principal one has hitherto escaped detection; at least, in the discussions on the subject, either in print or conversation, which have fallen within my knowledge, the cause, which I conceive to have operated most strongly towards increasing the price of the necessaries of life, has not yet been suggested. There are some disorders, which, though they scarcely admit of a cure, or even of any considerable mitigation, are still capable of being made greatly worse. In such misfortunes it is of great importance to know the desperate nature of the disease. The next step to the alleviation of pain, is the bearing it with composure, and not aggravating it by impatience and irritation.

It cannot admit of a doubt with persons of sense and information, that, during the last year, there was a scarcity, to a certain extent, of all sorts of grain; but it must be at the same time acknowledged, that the price was higher than the degree of that scarcity would at first sight appear to warrant.

In the summer of 1799, in the course of a northern tour, I passed through Sweden. There was at that time a general dearth of corn throughout the country, owing to a long drought the preceding year. In the province of Wurmland, adjoining to Norway, it approached almost to a famine, and the lower classes of people suffered most severe distress. At the time we were passing through that part of the country, which was in July, they were reduced to two most miserable substitutes for bread; one, made of the inner bark of the fir, and the other, of the common sorrel dried, and powdered. These substances, though made into the usual shape of their rye bread, had no affinity to it whatever in taste, and but very little, I believe, in nourishment, as the effects of this

1

miserable food were but too visible in their pallid and unhealthy countenances.

There could be little doubt, that the degree of scarcity then prevailing in that part of Sweden, was considerably greater than any we have hitherto experienced here; and yet, as far as we could learn, the price of rye, which is the grain principally used for bread, had not risen above double its usual average; whereas in this country last year, in a scarcity, that must be acknowledged to be very greatly inferior in degree, wheat rose to above three times its former price.

The continuation of extraordinary high prices, after a harvest that was at one time looked forward to as abundant, has contributed still more to astonish and perplex the public mind. Many men of sense have joined in the universal cry of the common people, that there must be roguery somewhere; and the general indignation has fallen upon monopolizers, forestallers, and regraters-words, that are vented from every mouth with fearful execrations, and are applied indiscriminately to all middle men whatever, to every kind of trader that goes between the grower of the commodity and the consumer.

This popular clamour, headed by the Lord Chief Justice, and enforced throughout the country by the instructions of the grand juries, must make every reflecting mind tremble for the future supply of our markets. I cannot but think therefore, that I should do an acceptable service, if I could succeed in accounting for the present high price of the necessaries of life, without criminating a class of men, who, I believe, have been accused unjustly, and who, every political economist must know, are absolutely necessary in the complicated machinery that distributes the provisions and other commodities of a large nation.

I ought first to premise, however, that I am not interested in this question, further than as a lover of truth, and a well-wisher to my country. I have no sort of connection whatever with any of these middle men or great farmers, who are now the objects of public indignation: and, as an individual with a small fixed income, I am certainly among that class of persons on whom the high price of provisions must fall the heaviest.

To proceed to the point: I am most strongly inclined to suspect, that the attempt in most parts of the kingdom to increase the parish allowances in proportion to the price of corn, combined with the riches of the country, which have enabled it to proceed as far as it has done in this attempt, is, comparatively speaking, the sole cause, which has occasioned the price of provisions in this country to rise so much higher than the degree of scarcity would seem to warrant, so much higher than it would do in any other country where this cause did not operate.

It may appear, perhaps, at first, to the reader, that this cause is inadequate to the effect we experience; but, if he will kindly allow me a few minutes of patient and candid attention, I hope I shall be able to convince him, that it is not only adequate to produce the present high price of provisions of which we complain; but, admitting a real scarcity, that the attempt to carry it actually into execution, might raise the quartern loaf before the expiration of a year, to as many shillings as it is now pence.

Adam Smith has most justly stated, that the actual price at which a commodity is sold, is compounded of its natural price, the price at which it can be brought to market, allowing the usual profit in times of moderate plenty, and the proportion of the supply to the demand. When any commodity is scarce, its natural price is necessarily forgotten, and its actual price is regulated by the excess of the demand above the supply.

Let us suppose a commodity in great request by fifty people, but of which, from some failure in its production, there is only sufficient to supply forty. If the fortieth man from the top have two shillings which he can spend in this commodity, and the thirty nine above him, more, in various proportions, and the ten below, all less, the actual price of the article, according to the genuine principles of trade, will be two shillings. If more be asked, the whole will not be sold, because there are only forty who have as much as two shillings to spend in the article; and there is no reason for asking less, because the whole may be disposed of at that sum.

Let us suppose, now, that somebody gives the ten poor men, who were excluded, a shilling apiece. The whole fifty can now offer two shillings, the price which was before asked. According to every genuine principle of fair trading, the commodity must immediately rise. If it do not, I would ask, upon what principle are ten, out of the fifty who are all able to offer two shillings, to be rejected? For still, according to the supposition there is only enough for forty. The two shillings of a poor man are just as good as the two shillings of a rich one; and, if we interfere to prevent the commodity from rising out of the reach of the poorest ten, whoever they may be, we must toss up, draw lots, raffle, or fight, to determine who are to be excluded. It would be beyond my present purpose, to enter into the question whether any of these modes would be more eligible, for the distribution of the commodities

3

of a country, than the sordid distinction of money; but certainly, according to the customs of all civilized and enlightened nations, and according to every acknowledged principle of commercial dealing, the price must be allowed to rise to that point which will put it beyond the power of ten out of the fifty to purchase. This point will, perhaps, be half a crown or more, which will now become the price of the commodity. Let another shilling apiece be given to the excluded ten: All will now be able to offer half a crown. The price must in consequence immediately rise to three shillings or more, and so on *toties quoties*.

In the progress of this operation the ten excluded would not be always entirely the same. The richest of the ten first excluded, would probably be raised above the poorest of the first forty. Small changes of this kind must take place. The additional allowances to the poorest, and the weight of the high prices on those above them, would tend to level the two orders; but, till a complete level had taken place, ten must be always excluded, and the price would always be fixed, as nearly as possible, at that sum which the fortieth man at the top could afford to give. This, if the donatives were continued, would raise the commodity to an extraordinary price, without the supposition of any combination and conspiracy among the vendors, or any kind of unfair dealing whatever.

The rise in the price of corn, and of other provisions, in this country, has been effected exactly in the same manner, though the operation may be a little more complicated; and I am firmly convinced, that it never could have reached its present height, but from the system of poor laws and parish allowances, which have operated precisely in the same mode as the donatives of a shilling in the instance I have just adduced.

The harvest of 1799 was bad, both in quality and quantity. Few people could deny that there appeared to be a very considerable deficiency of produce: And the price of the load of wheat rose in consequence almost immediately to £20. I returned from the north in the beginning of November, and found the alarm so great and general, and the price of corn so high, that I remember thinking that it was probably fully adequate to the degree of the deficiency, and, taking into consideration the prospect of importation from the very early alarm, that it would not rise much higher during the year. In this conjecture, it appears that I was much mistaken; but I have very little doubt that in any other country equally rich, yet without the system of poor laws and parish allowances, the price would never have exceeded £25 the load of wheat; and that this sum would have been sufficiently high to have excluded such a number of people from their usual consumption, as to make the deficient crop, with the quantity imported, last throughout the year.

The system of poor laws, and parish allowances, in this country, and I will add, to their honour, the humanity and generosity of the higher and middle classes of society, naturally and necessarily altered this state of things. The poor complained to the justices that their wages would not enable them to supply their families in the single article of bread. The justices very humanely, and I am far from saying improperly, listened to their complaints, inquired what was the smallest sum on which they could support their families, at the then price of wheat, and gave an order of relief on the parish accordingly. The poor were now enabled, for a short time, to purchase nearly their usual quantity of flour; but the stock in the country was not sufficient, even with the prospect of importation, to allow of the usual distribution to all its members. The crop was consuming too fast. Every market day the demand exceeded the supply; and those whose business it was to judge on these subjects, felt convinced, that in a month or two the scarcity would be greater than it was at that time. Those who were able, therefore, kept back their corn. In so doing, they undoubtedly consulted their own interest; but they, as undoubtedly, whether with the intention or not is of no consequence, consulted the true interest of the state: for, if they had not kept it back, too much would have been consumed, and there would have been a famine instead of a scarcity at the end of the year.

The corn, therefore, naturally rose. The poor were again distressed. fresh complaints were made to the justices, and a further relief granted; but, like the water from the mouth of Tantalus, the corn still slipped from the grasp of the poor; and rose again so as to disable them from purchasing a sufficiency to keep their families in health. The alarm now became still greater, and more general.[1] The justices in their individual capacities were not thought competent to determine on the proper modes of relief in the present crisis, a general meeting of the magistrates was called, aided by the united wisdom of other gentlemen of the county; but the result was merely the continuation and extension of the former system of relief; and, to say the truth, I hardly see what else could have been done. In some parishes this relief was given in the shape of flour; in others, which was certainly better, in money, accompanied with a recommendation not to spend the whole of it in wheaten bread, but to adopt some other kind of food. All, however, went upon the principle of inquiring what was the usual consumption of flour in the different families, and of enabling them to purchase nearly the same quantity that they did before the scarcity. With this additional command of money in the lower classes, and the consequent increased consumption, the number of purchasers at the then price would naturally exceed the supply. The corn would in consequence continue rising. The poor's rates in many parishes increased from four shillings in the pound to fourteen; the price of wheat necessarily kept pace with them; and before the end of the year was at near £40 a load; when probably without the operation of this cause it would not have exceeded £20 or £25.

Some of the poor would naturally make use of their additional command of money to purchase butter, cheese, bacon, pickled pork, rice, potatoes, etc. These commodities are all more limited in quantity than corn; and would, therefore, more suddenly feel the increased demand. If butter, cheese, bacon, pickled pork, and the coarser parts of meat, had continued at their usual price, they would have been purchased by so many, to come in aid of an inferior kind of bread, or to give a relish and additional nourishment to their potatoes and rice, that the supply would not have been half adequate to the quantity of these articles that were wanted. These commodities, therefore, rose as naturally and as necessarily as the corn; and, according to the genuine principles of fair trade, their price was fixed at that sum which only such a number could afford to give, as would enable the supply to answer the demand.

To fix upon this sum is the great object of every dealer and speculator in every commodity whatever, and about which he must, of course, exercise his private judgment. A reflecting mind, far from being astonished that there are now and then errors in speculation, must feel much greater astonishment that there are so few; and that the supplies of a large nation, whether plentiful or scanty, should be distributed so equally throughout the year. Most happily for society, individual interest is, in these cases, so closely and intimately interwoven with the public interest, that one cannot gain or lose without a gain or loss to the other. The man who refuses to send his corn to market when it is at £20 a load, because he thinks that in two months' time it will be at £30, if he be right in his judgment, and succeed in his speculation, is a positive and decided benefactor to the state; because he keeps his supply to that period when the state is much more in want of it; and if he and some others did not keep it back in that manner, instead of its being £30 in two months, it would be £40 or £50.

If he be wrong in his speculation, he loses perhaps very considerably himself, and the state suffers a little; because, had he brought his corn to market at £20, the price would have fallen sooner, and the event showed that there was corn enough in the country to allow of it: But the slight evil that the state suffers in this case is almost wholly compensated by the glut in the market, when the corn is brought out, which makes the price fall below what it would have been otherwise.

I am far from saying that there can be no such thing as monopoly, and the other hard words that have been so much talked of. In a commodity of a confined nature, within the purchase of two or three large capitals, or of a company of merchants, we all know that it has often existed; and, in a very few instances, the article may have been in part destroyed, to enhance the price, as the Dutch Company destroyed the nutmeg trees in their spice islands: but in an article which is in so many hands as corn is, in this country, monopoly, to any pernicious extent, may safely be pronounced impossible. Where are the capitals, or where is the company of merchants, rich enough to buy such a quantity of corn, as would make it answer to them to destroy, or, which is the same thing, not to sell a great part of it? As they could not, by the greatest of exertions, purchase one fourth of all the corn in the country, it is evident that, if any considerable part of their stock remained unsold, they would have enriched all the other dealers in corn at their own expense; and would not have gained half so much in proportion to their capital as the rest of the farmers and cornfactors. If on the contrary all their stock sold, it would be a proof that the speculation had been just, and that the country had really benefited by it.

It seems now to be universally agreed, that the stock of old corn remaining on hand at the beginning of the harvest this year was unusually small, notwithstanding that the harvest came on nearly a month sooner than could have been expected in the beginning of June. This is a clear, decided, and unanswerable proof that there had been no speculations in corn that were prejudicial to the country. All that the large farmers and cornfactors had done, was to raise the corn to that price which excluded a sufficient number from their usual consumption, to enable the supply to last throughout the year. This price, however, has been most essentially and powerfully affected by the ability that has been given to the labouring poor, by means of parish allowances, of continuing to purchase wheat notwithstanding its extraordinary rise:

And this ability must necessarily prevent the price of corn from falling very materially, till there is an actual glut in the market; for, while the whole stock will go off at £30 a load, it cannot, on any regular principle of trade, sink lower. I was in very great hopes, just before the harvest, that such a glut was about to take place; but it is now to be feared, from the nature of the present crop, that no such happy event can be hoped for during the year.

I do not know whether I have convinced my reader that the cause which I have assigned of the present extraordinary price of provisions is adequate to the effect; but I certainly feel most strongly convinced of it myself; and I cannot but believe that, if he differ from me, it can only be in degree, and from thinking that the principle of parish allowances has not yet been carried far enough to produce any material effect. With regard to the principle itself, if it were really carried into execution, it appears to me capable almost of mathematical demonstration, that, granting a real scarcity of one fourth, which could not be remedied by importation, it is adequate to the effecting any height of price that the proportion of the circulating medium to the quantity of corn daily consumed would admit.

It has often been proposed, and more than once I believe, in the House of Commons, to proportion the price of labour exactly to the price of provisions. This, though it would be always a bad plan, might pass tolerably in years of moderate plenty, or in a country that was in the habit of a considerable exportation of grain. But let us see what would be its operation in a real scarcity. We suppose, for the sake of the argument, that by law every kind of labour is to be paid accurately in proportion to the price of corn, and that the rich are to be assessed to the utmost to support those in the same manner who are thrown out of employment, and fall upon the parish. We allow the scarcity to be an irremediable deficiency of one fourth of all the provisions of the country. It is evident that, notwithstanding this deficiency, there would be no reason for economy in the labouring classes. The rise of their wages, or the parish allowances that they would receive, would enable them to purchase exactly the same quantity of corn, or other provisions, that they did before, whatever their price might be. The same quantity would of course be consumed; and, according to the regular principles of trade, as the stock continued diminishing, the price of all the necessaries of life would continue rising, in the most rapid and unexampled manner. The middle classes of society would very soon be blended with the poor; and the largest fortunes could not stand against the accumulated pressure of the extraordinary price of provisions, on the one hand, and the still more extraordinary assessments for allowances to those who had no other means of support, on the other. The corn-factors and farmers would undoubtedly be the last that suffered, but, at the expiration of the three quarters of a year, what they received with one hand, they must give away with the other; and a most complete levelling of all property would take place. All would have the same quantity of money. All the provisions of the country would be consumed: And all the people would starve together.

There is no kind of fear, that any such tragical event should ever happen in any country; but I allowed myself to make the supposition; because, it appears to me, that, in the complicated machinery of human society, the effect of any particular principle frequently escapes from the view, even of an attentive observer, if it be not magnified by pushing it to extremity.

I do not, however, by any means, intend to infer, from what I have said, that the parish allowances have been prejudicial to the state; or that, as far as the system has been hitherto pursued, or is likely to be pursued, in this country, that it is not one of the best modes of relief that the circumstances of the case will admit. The system of the poor laws, in general, I certainly do most heartily condemn, as I have expressed in another place, but I am inclined to think that their operation in the present scarcity has been advantageous to the country. The principal benefit which they have produced, is exactly that which is most bitterly complained of the high price of all the necessaries of life. The poor cry out loudly at this price; but, in so doing, they are very little aware of what they are about; for it has undoubtedly been owing to this price that a much greater number of them has not been starved.

It was calculated that there were only two thirds of an average crop last year. Probably, even with the aid of all that we imported, the deficiency still remained a fifth or sixth. Supposing ten millions of people in the island; the whole of this deficiency, had things been left to their natural course, would have fallen almost exclusively on two, or perhaps three millions of the poorest inhabitants, a very considerable number of whom must in consequence have starved. The operation of the parish allowances, by raising the price of provisions so high, caused the distress to be divided among five or six millions, perhaps, instead of two or three, and to be by no means unfelt even by the remainder of the population.

9

The high price, therefore, which is so much complained of by the poor, has essentially mitigated their distress by bringing down to their level two or three millions more, and making them almost equal sharers in the pressure of the scarcity.

The further effects of the high price have been to enforce a strict economy in all ranks of life; to encourage an extraordinary importation, and to animate the farmer by the powerful motive of self-interest to make every exertion to obtain as great a crop as possible the next year.

If economy, importation, and every possible encouragement to future production, have not the fairest chance of putting an end to the scarcity, I confess myself at a loss to say what better means can be substituted. I may undoubtedly on this subject be much mistaken; but to me, I own, they appear more calculated to answer the purpose intended, than the hanging any number of farmers and cornfactors that could be named.

No inference, therefore, is meant to be drawn against what has been done for the relief of the poor in the present scarcity, though it has without doubt greatly raised the price of provisions. All that I contend for is, that we should be aware of the effect of what we ourselves have done, and not lay the blame on the wrong persons.

If the cause, which I have detailed, be sufficient to account for the present high price of provisions, without the supposition of any unfair dealing among the farmers and cornfactors, we ought surely to bear the present pressure like men labouring under a disorder that must have its course, and not throw obstacles in the way of returning plenty, and endanger the future supplies of our markets, by encouraging the popular clamour, and keeping the farmers and corn dealers in perpetual fear for their lives and property.

To suppose that a year of scarcity can pass without distressing severely a large part of the inhabitants of a country, is to suppose a contradiction in the nature of things. I know of no other definition of a scarcity than the failure of the usual quantity of provisions; and if a great part of the people had but just enough before, they must undoubtedly have less than enough at such a period. With regard to the scarcity being artificial, it appears to me so impossible, that, till it has been proved that some man or set of men, with a capital of twenty or thirty millions sterling, has bought up half the corn in the country, I own I must still disbelieve it. On this subject, however, I know that I differ from some very respectable friends of mine, among the common people, who say that it is quite impossible that there can be a real scarcity, because you may get what quantity of corn you please, if you have but money enough; and to say the truth, many persons, who ought to be better informed, argue exactly in the same way. I have often talked with labouring men on this subject, and endeavored to show them, that if they, or I, had a great deal of money, and other people had but little, we could undoubtedly buy what quantity of corn we liked, by taking away the shares of those who were less rich; but that if all the people had the same sum, and that there was not enough corn in the country to supply all, we could not get what we wanted for money, though we possessed millions. I never found, however, that my rhetoric produced much impression.

The cry at present is in favour of small farms, and against middle men. No two clamours can well be more inconsistent with each other, as the destruction of the middle men would, I conceive, necessarily involve with it the destruction of small farmers. The small farmer requires a quick return of his scanty capital to enable him to pay his rent and his workmen; and must therefore send his corn to market almost immediately after harvest. If he were required to perform the office of corn dealer, as well as farmer, and wait to regulate his supplies to the demands of the markets, a double capital would be absolutely necessary to him, and not having that, he would be ruined.

Many men of sense and information have attributed the dearness of provisions to the quantity of paper in circulation. There was undoubtedly great reason for apprehension, that when, by the stoppage of the Bank to pay in specie, the emission of paper ceased to have its natural check, the circulation would be overloaded with this currency; but this certainly could not have taken place to any considerable extent without a sensible depreciation of bank notes in comparison with specie. As this depreciation did not happen, the progress of the evil must have been slow and gradual, and never could have produced the sudden and extraordinary rise in the price of provisions which was so sensibly felt last year, after a season of moderate cheapness, subsequent to the stoppage of the Bank.

There is one circumstance, however, that ought to be attended to. To circulate the same, or nearly the same,[2] quantity of commodities through a country, when they bear a much higher price, must require a greater quantity of the medium, whatever that may be. The circulation naturally takes up more. It is probable, therefore, that the Bank has found it necessary to issue a greater number of its notes on this account. Or, if it has not, this deficiency has been supplied by the country bankers, who have found that their notes now stay out longer, and in greater quantity, than they did before the scarcity, which may tempt many to overtrade their capitals. If the quantity of paper, therefore, in circulation has greatly increased during the last year, I should be inclined to consider it rather as the effect than the cause of the high price of provisions. This fullness of circulating medium, however, will be one of the obstacles in the way to returning cheapness.

The public attention is now fixed with anxiety towards the meeting of Parliament, which is to relieve us from our present difficulties; but the more considerate do not feel very sanguine on this subject, knowing how little is to be done in this species of distress by legislative interference. We interfere to fix the assize of bread. Perhaps one of the best interferences of the legislature, in the present instance, would be to abolish that assize. I have certainly no tendency to believe in combinations and conspiracies; but the great interval that elapses between the fall of wheat and the fall of flour, compared with the quick succession of the rise of flour to the rise of wheat, would almost tempt one to suppose, that there might be some little management in the return of the meal weighers to the Lord Mayor. If the public suffer in this instance, it is evidently owing to the assize, without which, the opportunity of any such management would not exist. And what occasion can there be for an assize in a city like London, in which there are so many bakers? If such a regulation were ever necessary, it would appear to be most so in a country village or small town, where perhaps there is but one person in the trade, and who might, therefore, for a time, have an opportunity of imposing on his customers; but this could not take place where there was such room for competition as in London. If there were no assize, more attention would be constantly paid to the weight and quality of the bread bought; and the bakers who sold the best in these two respects would have the most custom. The removal of this regulation would remove, in a great measure, the difficulty about brown bread, and a much greater quantity of it would probably be consumed.

The soup shops, and every attempt to make a nourishing and palatable food of what was before not in use among the common people, must evidently be of great service in the present distress.

It is a fact now generally acknowledged, and it has lately received an official sanction in a letter of the Duke of Portland to the Lord Lieutenant of the county of Oxford, that of late years, even in the best seasons, we have not grown corn sufficient for our own consumption; whereas, twenty years ago, we were in the constant habit of exporting grain to a very considerable amount. Though we may suppose that the agriculture of the country has not been increasing, as it ought to have done, during this period; yet we cannot well imagine that it has gone backwards. To what then can we attribute the present inability in the country to support its inhabitants, but to the increase of population? I own that I cannot but consider the late severe pressures of distress on every deficiency in our crops, as a very strong exemplification of a principle which I endeavored to explain in an essay published about two years ago, entitled, *An Essay on the Principle of Population*, as it affects the future improvement of society. It was considered by many who read it, merely as a specious argument, inapplicable to the present state of society; because it contradicted some preconceived opinions on these subjects. Two years' reflection have, however, served strongly to convince me of the truth of the principle there advanced, and of its being the real cause of the continued depression and poverty of the lower classes of society, of the total inadequacy of all the present establishments in their favour to relieve them, and of the periodical returns of such seasons of distress as we have of late experienced.

The essay has now been out of print above a year; but I have deferred giving another edition of it in the hope of being able to make it more worthy of the public attention, by applying the principle directly and exclusively to the existing state of society, and endeavoring to illustrate the power and universality of its operation from the best authenticated accounts that we have of the state of other countries. Particular engagements in the former part of the time, and some most unforeseen and unfortunate interruptions latterly, have hitherto prevented me from turning my attention, with any effect, towards this subject. I still, however, have it in view. In the meantime I hope that this hasty attempt to add my mite to the public stock of information, in the present emergency, will be received with candour.

Notes

1. I am describing what took place in the neighbourhood where I then lived, and I have reason to believe that something nearly similar took place in most counties of the kingdom.

2. In a scarcity the quantity of commodities in circulation is probably not so great as in years of plenty.

Observations on the Effects of the Corn Laws, and of a Rise or Fall in the Price of Corn on the Agriculture and General Wealth of the Country

T.R. Malthus; 1814

A revision of the corn laws, it is understood, is immediately to come under the consideration of the legislature. That the decision on such a subject, should be founded on a correct and enlightened view of the whole question, will be allowed to be of the utmost importance, both with regard to the stability of the measures to be adopted, and the effects to be expected from them.

For an attempt to contribute to the stock of information necessary to form such a decision, no apology can be necessary. It may seem indeed probable, that but little further light can be thrown on a subject, which, owing to the system adopted in this country, has been so frequently the topic of discussion; but, after the best consideration which I have been able to give it, I own, it appears to me, that some important considerations have been neglected on both sides of the question, and that the effects of the corn laws, and of a rise or fall in the price of corn, on the agriculture and general wealth of the state, have not yet been fully laid before the public.

If this be true, I cannot help attributing it in some degree to the very peculiar argument brought forward by Dr. Smith, in his discussion of the bounty upon the exportation of corn. Those who are conversant with the *Wealth of Nations*, will be aware, that its great author has, on this occasion, left entirely in the background the broad, grand, and almost unanswerable arguments, which the general principles of political economy furnish in abundance against all systems of bounties and restrictions, and has only brought forwards, in a prominent manner, one which, it is intended, should apply to corn alone. It is not surprising that so high an authority should have had the effect of attracting the attention of the advocates of each side of the question, in an especial manner, to this particular argument. Those who have maintained the same cause with Dr. Smith, have treated it nearly in the same way; and, though they may have alluded to the other more general and legitimate arguments against bounties and restrictions, have almost universally seemed to place their chief reliance on the appropriate and particular argument relating to the nature of corn.

On the other hand, those who have taken the opposite side of the question, if they have imagined that they had combated this particular argument with success, have been too apt to consider the point as determined, without much reference to the more weighty and important arguments, which remained behind.

Among the latter description of persons I must rank myself. I have always thought, and still think, that this peculiar argument of Dr. Smith, is fundamentally erroneous, and that it cannot be maintained without violating the great principles of supply and demand, and contradicting the general spirit and scope of the reasonings, which pervade the *Wealth of Nations*.

But I am most ready to confess, that, on a former occasion, when I considered the corn laws, my attention was too much engrossed by this one peculiar view of the subject, to give the other arguments, which belong to it, their due weight.

I am anxious to correct an error, of which I feel conscious. It is not however my intention, on the present occasion, to express an opinion on the general question. I shall only endeavor to state, with the strictest impartiality, what appear to me to be the advantages and disadvantages of each system, in the actual circumstances of our present situation, and what are the specific consequences, which may be expected to result from the adoption of either. My main object is to assist in affording the materials for a just and enlightened decision; and, whatever that decision may be, to prevent disappointment, in the event of the effects of the measure not being such as were previously contemplated. Nothing would tend so powerfully to bring the general principles of political economy into disrepute, and to prevent their spreading, as their being supported upon any occasion by reasoning, which constant and unequivocal experience should afterwards prove to be fallacious.

We must begin, therefore, by an inquiry into the truth of Dr. Smith's argument, as we cannot with propriety proceed to the main question, till this preliminary point is settled.

The substance of his argument is, that corn is of so peculiar a nature, that its real price cannot be raised by an increase of its money price; and that, as it is clearly an increase of real price alone which can encourage its production, the rise of money price, occasioned by a bounty, can have no such effect.

It is by no means intended to deny the powerful influence of the price of corn upon the price of labour, on an average of a considerable number of years; but that this influence is not such as to prevent the movement of capital to, or from the land, which is the precise point in question, will be made sufficiently evident by a short inquiry into the manner in which labour is paid and brought into the market, and by a consideration of the consequences to which the assumption of Dr. Smith's proposition would inevitably lead.

In the first place, if we inquire into the expenditure of the labouring classes of society, we shall find, that it by no means consists wholly in food, and still less, of course, in mere bread or grain. In looking over that mine of information, for everything relating to prices and labour, Sir Frederick Morton Eden's work on the poor, I find, that in a labourer's family of about an average size, the articles of house rent, fuel, soap, candles, tea, sugar, and clothing, are generally equal to the articles of bread or meal. On a very rough estimate, the whole may be divided into five parts, of which two consist of meal or bread, two of the articles above mentioned, and one of meat, milk, butter, cheese, and potatoes. These divisions are, of course, subject to considerable variations, arising from the number of the family, and the amount of the earnings. But if they merely approximate towards the truth, a rise in the price of corn must be both slow and partial in its effects upon labour. Meat, milk, butter, cheese, and potatoes are slowly affected by the price of corn; house rent, bricks, stone, timber, fuel, soap, candles, and clothing, still more slowly; and, as far as some of them depend, in part or in the whole, upon foreign materials (as is the case with leather, linen, cottons, soap, and candles), they may be considered as independent of it; like the two remaining articles of tea and sugar, which are by no means unimportant in their amount.

It is manifest therefore that the whole of the wages of labour can never rise and fall in proportion to the variations in the price of grain. And that the effect produced by these variations, whatever may be its amount, must be very slow in its operation, is proved by the manner in which the supply of labour takes place; a point, which has been by no means sufficiently attended to.

Every change in the prices of commodities, if left to find their natural level, is occasioned by some change, actual or expected, in the state of the demand or supply. The reason why the consumer pays a tax upon any manufactured commodity, or an advance in the price of any of its component parts, is because, if he cannot or will not pay this advance of price, the commodity will not be supplied in the same quantity as before; and the next year there will only be such a proportion in the market, as is accommodated to the number of persons who will consent to pay the tax. But, in the case of labour, the operation of withdrawing the commodity is much slower and more painful. Although the purchasers refuse to pay the advanced price, the same supply will necessarily remain in the market, not only the next year, but for some years to come. Consequently, if no increase take place in the demand, and the advanced price of provisions be not so great, as to make it obvious that the labourer cannot support his family, it is probable, that he will continue to pay this advance, till a relaxation in the rate of the increase of population causes the market to be under-supplied with labour; and then, of course, the competition among the purchasers will raise the price above the proportion of the advance, in order to restore the supply. In the same manner, if an advance in the price of labour has taken place during two or three years of great scarcity, it is probable that, on the return of plenty, the real recompense of labour will continue higher than the usual average, till a too rapid increase of population causes a competition among the labourers, and a consequent diminution of the price of labour below the usual rate.

This account of the manner in which the price of corn may be expected to operate upon the price of labour, according to the laws which regulate the progress of population, evidently shows, that corn and labour rarely keep an even pace together; but must often be separated at a sufficient distance and for a sufficient time, to change the direction of capital.

As a further confirmation of this truth, it may be useful to consider, secondly, the consequences to which the assumption of Dr. Smith's proposition would inevitably lead.

If we suppose, that the real price of corn is unchangeable, or not capable of experiencing a relative increase or decrease of value, compared with labour and other commodities, it will follow, that agriculture is at once excluded from the operation of that principle, so beautifully explained and illustrated by Dr. Smith, by which capital flows from one employment to another, according to the various and necessarily fluctuating wants of society. It will follow, that the growth of corn has, at all times, and in all countries, proceeded with a uniform unvarying pace, occasioned only by the equable increase of agricultural capital, and can never have been accelerated, or retarded, by variations of demand. It will follow, that if a country happened to be either overstocked or understocked with corn, no motive of interest could exist for withdrawing capital from agriculture, in the one case, or adding to it in the other, and thus restoring the equilibrium between its different kinds of produce. But these consequences, which would incontestably follow from the doctrine, that the price of corn immediately and entirely regulates the prices of labour and of all other commodities, are so directly contrary to all experience, that the doctrine itself cannot possibly be true; and we may be assured, that, whatever influence the price of corn may have upon other commodities, it is neither so immediate nor so complete, as to make this kind of produce an exception to all others.

That no such exception exists with regard to corn, is implied in all the general reasonings of the *Wealth of Nations*. Dr. Smith evidently felt this; and wherever, in consequence, he does not shift the question from the exchangeable value of corn to its physical properties, he speaks with an unusual want of precision, and qualifies his positions by the expressions much, and in any considerable degree. But it should be recollected, that, with these qualifications, the argument is brought forward expressly for the purpose of showing, that the rise of price, acknowledged to be occasioned by a bounty, on its first establishment, is nominal and not real. Now, what is meant to be distinctly asserted here is, that a rise of price occasioned by a bounty upon the exportation or restrictions upon the importation of corn, cannot be less real than a rise of price to the same amount, occasioned by a course of bad seasons, an increase of population, the rapid progress of commercial wealth, or any other natural cause; and that, if Dr. Smith's argument, with its qualifications, be valid for the purpose for which it is advanced, it applies equally to an increased price occasioned by a natural demand.

Let us suppose, for instance, an increase in the demand and the price of corn, occasioned by an unusually prosperous state of our manufactures and foreign commerce; a fact which has frequently come within our own experience. According to the principles of supply and demand, and the general principles of the *Wealth of Nations*, such an increase in the price of corn would give a decided stimulus to agriculture; and a more than usual quantity of capital would be laid out upon the land, as appears obviously to have been the case in this country during the last twenty years. According to the peculiar argument of Dr. Smith, however, no such stimulus could have been given

19

to agriculture. The rise in the price of corn would have been immediately followed by a proportionate rise in the price of labour and of all
other commodities; and, though the farmer and landlord might have
obtained, on an average, seventy-five shillings a quarter for their corn,
instead of sixty, yet the farmer would not have been enabled to cultivate better, nor the landlord to live better. And thus it would appear,
that agriculture is beyond the operation of that principle, which distributes the capital of a nation according to the varying profits of stock
in different employments; and that no increase of price can, at any time
or in any country, materially accelerate the growth of corn, or determine a greater quantity of capital to agriculture.

The experience of every person, who sees what is going forward on
the land, and the feelings and conduct both of farmers and landlords,
abundantly contradict this reasoning.

Dr. Smith was evidently led into this train of argument, from his
habit of considering labour as the standard measure of value, and corn
as the measure of labour. But, that corn is a very inaccurate measure of
labour, the history of our own country will amply demonstrate; where
labour, compared with corn, will be found to have experienced very
great and striking variations, not only from year to year, but from century to century; and for ten, twenty, and thirty years together;[1] and that
neither labour nor any other commodity can be an accurate measure of
real value in exchange, is now considered as one of the most incontro-
vertible doctrines of political economy, and indeed follows, as a necessary consequence, from the very definition of value in exchange. But
to allow that corn regulates the prices of all commodities, is at once to
erect it into a standard measure of real value in exchange; and we must
either deny the truth of Dr. Smith's argument, or acknowledge, that
what seems to be quite impossible is found to exist; and that a given
quantity of corn, notwithstanding the fluctuations to which its supply
and demand must be subject, and the fluctuations to which the supply
and demand of all the other commodities with which it is compared
must also be subject, will, on the average of a few years, at all times and
in all countries, purchase the same quantity of labour and of the
necessaries and conveniences of life.

There are two obvious truths in political economy, which have not
infrequently been the sources of error.

It is undoubtedly true, that corn might be just as successfully cultivated, and as much capital might be laid out upon the land, at the
price of twenty shillings a quarter, as at the price of one hundred shil-

lings, provided that every commodity, both at home and abroad, were precisely proportioned to the reduced scale. In the same manner as it is strictly true, that the industry and capital of a nation would be exactly the same (with the slight exception at least of plate), if, in every exchange, both at home or abroad, one shilling only were used, where five are used now.

But to infer, from these truths, that any natural or artificial causes, which should raise or lower the values of corn or silver, might be considered as matters of indifference, would be an error of the most serious magnitude. Practically, no material change can take place in the value of either, without producing both lasting and temporary effects, which have a most powerful influence on the distribution of property, and on the demand and supply of particular commodities. The discovery of the mines of America, during the time that it raised the price of corn between three and four times, did not nearly so much as double the price of labour; and, while it permanently diminished the power of all fixed incomes, it gave a prodigious increase of power to all landlords and capitalists. In a similar manner, the fall in the price of corn, from whatever cause it took place, which occurred towards the middle of the last century, accompanied as it was by a rise, rather than a fall in the price of labour, must have given a great relative check to the employment of capital upon the land, and a great relative stimulus to population; a state of things precisely calculated to produce the reaction afterwards experienced, and to convert us from an exporting to an importing nation.

It is by no means sufficient for Dr. Smith's argument, that the price of corn should determine the price of labour under precisely the same circumstances of supply and demand. To make it applicable to his purpose, he must show, in addition, that a natural or artificial rise in the price of corn, or in the value of silver, will make no alteration in the state of property, and in the supply and demand of corn and labour; a position which experience uniformly contradicts.

Nothing then can be more evident both from theory and experience, than that the price of corn does not immediately and generally regulate the prices of labour and all other commodities; and that the real price of corn is capable of varying for periods of sufficient length to give a decided stimulus or discouragement to agriculture. It is, of course, only to a temporary encouragement or discouragement, that any commodity, where the competition is free, can be subjected. We may increase the capital employed either upon the land or in the cotton manufacture, but it is impossible permanently to raise the profits of farmers or particular manufacturers above the level of other profits; and, after the influx of a certain quantity of capital, they will necessarily be equalized. Corn, in this respect, is subjected to the same laws as other commodities, and the difference between them is by no means so great as stated by Dr. Smith.

In discussing, therefore, the present question, we must lay aside the peculiar argument relating to the nature of corn; and allowing that it is possible to encourage cultivation by corn laws, we must direct our chief attention to the question of the policy or impolicy of such a system.

While our great commercial prosperity continues, it is scarcely possible that we should become again an exporting nation with regard to corn. The bounty has long been a dead letter; and will probably remain so. We may at present then confine our inquiry to the restrictions upon the importation of foreign corn with a view to an independent supply.

The determination of the question, respecting the policy or impolicy of continuing the corn laws, seems to depend upon the three following points:

> First, Whether, upon the supposition of the most perfect freedom of importation and exportation, it is probable that Great Britain and Ireland would grow an independent supply of corn.
>
> Secondly, Whether an independent supply, if it does not come naturally, is an object really desirable, and one which justifies the interference of the legislature.
>
> And, Thirdly, If an independent supply be considered as such an object, how far, and by what sacrifices, are restrictions upon importation adapted to attain the end in view.

Of the first point, it may be observed, that it cannot, in the nature of things, be determined by general principles, but must depend upon the size, soil, facilities of culture, and demand for corn in the country in question. We know that it answers to almost all small well-peopled states, to import their corn; and there is every reason to suppose, that even a large landed nation, abounding in a manufacturing population, and having cultivated all its good soil, might find it cheaper to purchase a considerable part of its corn in other countries, where the supply, compared with the demand, was more abundant. If the intercourse between the different parts of Europe were perfectly easy and perfectly free, it would be by no means natural that one country should be employing a great capital in the cultivation of poor lands, while at no great distance, lands comparatively rich were lying very ill cultivated, from the want of an effectual demand. The progress of agricultural improvement ought naturally to proceed more equally. It is true, indeed, that the accumulation of capital, skill, and population in particular districts, might give some facilities of culture not possessed by poorer nations; but such facilities could not be expected to make up for great differences in the quality of the soil and the expenses of cultivation. And it is impossible to conceive that under very great inequalities in the demand for corn in different countries, occasioned by a very great difference in the accumulation of mercantile and manufacturing capital and in the number of large towns, an equalization of price could take place, without the transfer of a part of the general supply of Europe, from places where the demand was comparatively deficient, to those where it was comparatively excessive.

According to Oddy's *European Commerce*, the Poles can afford to bring their corn to Danzig at thirty-two shillings a quarter. The Baltic merchants are said to be of opinion that the price is not very different at present; and there can be little doubt, that if the corn growers in the neighbourhood of the Baltic could look forward to a permanently open market in the British ports, they would raise corn expressly for the purpose. The same observation is applicable to America; and under such circumstances it would answer to both countries, for many years to come, to afford us supplies of corn, in much larger quantities than we have ever yet received from them.

During the five years from 1804 to 1808, both inclusive, the bullion price of corn was about seventy-five shillings per quarter; yet, at this price, it answered to us better to import some portion of our supplies than to bring our land into such a state of cultivation as to grow our own consumption. We have already shown how slowly and partially the price of corn affects the price of labour and some of the other expenses of cultivation. Is it credible, then, that if by the freedom of importation the prices of corn were equalized, and reduced to about forty-five or fifty shillings a quarter, it could answer to us to go on improving our agriculture with our increasing population, or even to maintain our produce in its actual state?

23

It is a great mistake to suppose that the effects of a fall in the price of corn on cultivation may be fully compensated by a diminution of rents. Rich land which yields a large net rent, may indeed be kept up in its actual state, notwithstanding a fall in the price of its produce: as a diminution of rent may be made entirely to compensate this fall and all the additional expenses that belong to a rich and highly taxed country. But in poor land, the fund of rent will often be found quite insufficient for this purpose. There is a good deal of land in this country of such a quality that the expenses of its cultivation, together with the outgoings of poor rates, tithes and taxes, will not allow the farmer to pay more than a fifth or sixth of the value of the whole produce in the shape of rent. If we were to suppose the prices of grain to fall from seventy-five shillings to fifty shillings the quarter, the whole of such a rent would be absorbed, even if the price of the whole produce of the farm did not fall in proportion to the price of grain, and making some allowance for a fall in the price of labour. The regular cultivation of such land for grain would of course be given up, and any sort of pasture, however scanty, would be more beneficial both to the landlord and farmer.

But a diminution in the real price of corn is still more efficient, in preventing the future improvement of land, than in throwing land, which has been already improved, out of cultivation. In all progressive countries, the average price of corn is never higher than what is necessary to continue the average increase of produce. And though, in much the greater part of the improved lands of most countries, there is what the French economists call a disposable produce, that is, a portion which might be taken away without interfering with future production, yet, in reference to the whole of the actual produce and the rate at which it is increasing, there is no part of the price so disposable. In the employment of fresh capital upon the land to provide for the wants of an increasing population, whether this fresh capital be employed in bringing more land under the plough or in improving land already in cultivation, the main question always depends upon the expected returns of this capital; and no part of the gross profits can be diminished without diminishing the motive to this mode of employing it. Every diminution of price not fully and immediately balanced by a proportionate fall in all the necessary expenses of a farm, every tax on the land, every tax on farming stock, every tax on the necessaries of farmers, will tell in the computation; and if, after all these outgoings are allowed for, the price of the produce will not leave a fair remuneration for the capital employed, according to the general rate of profits and a rent at least equal to the rent of the land in its former state, no sufficient motive can exist to undertake the projected improvement.

It was a fatal mistake in the system of the Economists to consider merely production and reproduction, and not the provision for an increasing population, to which their territorial tax would have raised the most formidable obstacles.

On the whole then considering the present accumulation of manufacturing population in this country, compared with any other in Europe, the expenses attending enclosures, the price of labour and the weight of taxes, few things seem less probable, than that Great Britain should naturally grow an independent supply of corn; and nothing can be more certain, than that if the prices of wheat in Great Britain were reduced by free importation nearly to a level with those of America and the continent, and if our manufacturing prosperity were to continue increasing, it would incontestably answer to us to support a part of our present population on foreign corn, and nearly the whole probably of the increasing population, which we may naturally expect to take place in the course of the next twenty or twenty-five years.

The next question for consideration is, whether an independent supply, if it does not come naturally, is an object really desirable and one which justifies the interference of the legislature.

The general principles of political economy teach us to buy all our commodities where we can have them the cheapest; and perhaps there is no general rule in the whole compass of the science to which fewer justifiable exceptions can be found in practice. In the simple view of present wealth, population, and power, three of the most natural and just objects of national ambition, I can hardly imagine an exception; as it is only by a strict adherence to this rule that the capital of a country can ever be made to yield its greatest amount of produce.

It is justly stated by Dr. Smith that by means of trade and manufactures a country may enjoy a much greater quantity of subsistence, and consequently may have a much greater population, than what its own lands could afford. If Holland, Venice, and Hamburg had declined a dependence upon foreign countries for their support, they would always have remained perfectly inconsiderable states, and never could have risen to that pitch of wealth, power, and population, which distinguished the meridian of their career.

Although the price of corn affects but slowly the price of labour, and never regulates it wholly, yet it has unquestionably a powerful influence upon it. A most perfect freedom of intercourse between different nations in the article of corn, greatly contributes to an equalization of prices and a level in the value of the precious metals. And it must be allowed that a country which possesses any peculiar facilities for successful exertion in manufacturing industry, can never make a full and complete use of its advantages; unless the price of its labour and other commodities be reduced to that level compared with other countries, which results from the most perfect freedom of the corn trade.

It has been sometimes urged as an argument in favour of the corn laws, that the great sums which the country has had to pay for foreign corn during the last twenty years must have been injurious to her resources, and might have been saved by the improvement of our agriculture at home. It might with just as much propriety be urged that we lose every year by our forty millions worth of imports, and that we should gain by diminishing these extravagant purchases. Such a doctrine cannot be maintained without giving up the first and most fundamental principles of all commercial intercourse. No purchase is ever made, either at home or abroad, unless that which is received is, in the estimate of the purchaser, of more value than that which is given; and we may rest quite assured, that we shall never buy corn or any other commodities abroad, if we cannot by so doing supply our wants in a more advantageous manner, and by a smaller quantity of capital, than if we had attempted to raise these commodities at home.

It may indeed occasionally happen that in an unfavourable season, our exchanges with foreign countries may be affected by the necessity of making unusually large purchases of corn; but this is in itself an evil of the slightest consequence, which is soon rectified, and in ordinary times is not more likely to happen, if our average imports were two millions of quarters, than if, on an average, we grew our own consumption.

The unusual demand is in this case the sole cause of the evil, and not the average amount imported. The habit on the part of foreigners of supplying this amount, would on the contrary rather facilitate than impede further supplies; and as all trade is ultimately a trade of barter, and the power of purchasing cannot be permanently extended without an extension of the power of selling, the foreign countries which supplied us with corn would evidently have their power of purchasing our commodities increased, and would thus contribute more effectually to our commercial and manufacturing prosperity.

It has further been intimated by the friends of the corn laws, that by growing our own consumption we shall keep the price of corn within moderate bounds and to a certain degree steady. But this also is an argument which is obviously not tenable; as in our actual situation, it is only by keeping the price of corn up, very considerably above the average of the rest of Europe, that we can possibly be made to grow our own consumption.

A bounty upon exportation in one country, may be considered, in some degree, as a bounty upon production in Europe; and if the growing price of corn in the country where the bounty is granted be not higher than in others, such a premium might obviously after a time have some tendency to create a temporary abundance of corn and a consequent fall in its price. But restrictions upon importation cannot have the slightest tendency of this kind. Their whole effect is to stint the supply of the general market, and to raise, not to lower, the price of corn.

Nor is it in their nature permanently to secure what is of more consequence, steadiness of prices. During the period indeed, in which the country is obliged regularly to import some foreign grain, a high duty upon it is effectual in steadily keeping up the price of home corn, and giving a very decided stimulus to agriculture. But as soon as the average supply becomes equal to the average consumption, this steadiness ceases. A plentiful year will occasion a sudden fall; and from the average price of the home produce being so much higher than in the other markets of Europe, such a fall can be but little relieved by exportation. It must be allowed, that a free trade in corn would in all ordinary cases not only secure a cheaper, but a more steady, supply of grain.

To counterbalance these striking advantages of a free trade in corn, what are the evils which are apprehended from it?

It is alleged, first, that security is of still more importance than wealth, and that a great country likely to excite the jealousy of others, if it become dependent for the support of any considerable portion of people upon foreign corn, exposes itself to the risk of having its most essential supplies suddenly fail at the time of its greatest need. That such a risk is not very great will be readily allowed. It would be as much against the interest of those nations which raised the superabundant supply as against the one which wanted it, that the intercourse should at any time be interrupted; and a rich country, which could afford to pay high for its corn, would not be likely to starve, while there was any to be purchased in the market of the commercial world.

At the same time it should be observed that we have latterly seen the most striking instances in all quarters, of governments acting from passion rather than interest. And though the recurrence of such a state of things is hardly to be expected, yet it must be allowed that if anything resembling it should take place in future, when, instead of very nearly growing our own consumption, we were indebted to foreign countries for the support of two million of our people, the distresses which our manufacturers suffered in 1812 would be nothing compared with the wide-wasting calamity which would be then experienced.

According to the returns made to Parliament in the course of the last session, the quantity of grain and flour exported in 1811 rather exceeded, than fell short of, what was imported; and in 1812, although the average price of wheat was one hundred and twenty-five shillings the quarter, the balance of the importations of grain and flour was only about one hundred thousand quarters. From 1805, partly from the operation of the corn laws passed in 1804, but much more from the difficulty and expense of importing corn in the actual state of Europe and America, the price of grain had risen so high and had given such a stimulus to our agriculture, that with the powerful assistance of Ireland, we had been rapidly approaching to the growth of an independent supply. Though the danger therefore may not be great of depending for a considerable portion of our subsistence upon foreign countries, yet it must be acknowledged that nothing like an experiment has yet been made of the distresses that might be produced, during a widely extended war, by the united operation, of a great difficulty in finding a market for our manufactures, accompanied by the absolute necessity of supplying ourselves with a very large quantity of corn.

Secondly, It may be said, that an excessive proportion of manufacturing population does not seem favourable to national quiet and happiness. Independently of any difficulties respecting the import of corn, variations in the channels of manufacturing industry and in the facilities of obtaining a vent for its produce are perpetually recurring. Not only during the last four or five years, but during the whole course of the war, have the wages of manufacturing labour been subject to great fluctuations. Sometimes they have been excessively high, and at other times proportionably low; and even during a peace they must always remain subject to the fluctuations which arise from the caprices of taste and fashion, and the competition of other countries. These fluctuations naturally tend to generate discontent and tumult and the evils which accompany them; and if to this we add, that the situation and employment of a manufacturer and his family are even in their best state unfavourable to health and virtue, it cannot appear desirable that a very large proportion of the whole society should consist of manufacturing labourers. Wealth, population and power are, after all, only valuable, as they tend to improve, increase, and secure the mass of human virtue and happiness.

Yet though the condition of the individual employed in common manufacturing labour is not by any means desirable, most of the effects of manufactures and commerce on the general state of society are in the highest degree beneficial. They infuse fresh life and activity into all classes of the state, afford opportunities for the inferior orders to rise by personal merit and exertion, and stimulate the higher orders to depend for distinction upon other grounds than mere rank and riches. They excite invention, encourage science and the useful arts, spread intelligence and spirit, inspire a taste for conveniences and comforts among the labouring classes; and, above all, give a new and happier structure to society, by increasing the proportion of the middle classes, that body on which the liberty, public spirit, and good government of every country must mainly depend.

If we compare such a state of society with a state merely agricultural, the general superiority of the former is incontestable; but it does not follow that the manufacturing system may not be carried to excess, and that beyond a certain point the evils which accompany it may not increase further than its advantages. The question, as applicable to this country, is not whether a manufacturing state is to be preferred to one merely agricultural, but whether a country the most manufacturing of any ever recorded in history, with an agriculture however as yet nearly keeping pace with it, would be improved in its happiness, by a great relative increase to its manufacturing population and relative check to its agricultural population.

Many of the questions both in morals and politics seem to be of the nature of the problems de maximis and minimis in fluxions; in which there is always a point where a certain effect is the greatest, while on either side of this point it gradually diminishes.

With a view to the permanent happiness and security from great reverses of the lower classes of people in this country, I should have little hesitation in thinking it desirable that its agriculture should keep pace with its manufactures, even at the expense of retarding in some degree the growth of manufactures; but it is a different question, whether it is wise to break through a general rule, and interrupt the natural course of things, in order to produce and maintain such an equalization.

Thirdly, It may be urged, that though a comparatively low value of the precious metals, or a high nominal price of corn and labour, tends rather to check commerce and manufactures, yet its effects are permanently beneficial to those who live by the wages of labour.

If the labourers in two countries were to earn the same quantity of corn, yet in one of them the nominal price of this corn were twenty-five per cent higher than in the other, the condition of the labourers where the price of corn was the highest, would be decidedly the best. In the purchase of all commodities purely foreign; in the purchase of those commodities, the raw materials of which are wholly or in part foreign, and therefore influenced in a great degree by foreign prices, and in the purchase of all home commodities which are taxed, and not taxed ad valorem, they would have an unquestionable advantage: And these articles altogether are not inconsiderable even in the expenditure of a cottager.

As one of the evils, therefore, attending the throwing open our ports, it may be stated, that if the stimulus to population, from the cheapness of grain, should in the course of twenty or twenty-five years reduce the earnings of the labourer to the same quantity of corn as at present, at the same price as in the rest of Europe, the condition of the lower classes of people in this country would be deteriorated. And if they should not be so reduced, it is quite clear that the encouragement to the growth of corn will not be fully restored, even after the lapse of so long a period.

Fourthly, It may be observed, that though it might by no means be advisable to commence an artificial system of regulations in the trade of corn; yet if, by such a system already established and other concurring causes, the prices of corn and of many commodities had been raised above the level of the rest of Europe, it becomes a different question, whether it would be advisable to risk the effects of so great and sudden a fall in the price of corn, as would be the consequence of at once throwing open our ports. One of the cases in which, according to Dr. Smith, "it may be a matter of deliberation how far it is proper to restore the free importation of foreign goods after it has been for some time interrupted, is, when particular manufactures, by means of high duties and prohibitions upon all foreign goods which can come into competition with them, have been so far extended as to employ a great multitude of hands."[2]

That the production of corn is not exempted from the operation of this rule has already been shown; and there can be no doubt that the interests of a large body of landholders and farmers, the former to a certain extent permanently, and the latter temporarily, would be deeply affected by such a change of policy. These persons too may further urge, with much appearance of justice, that in being made to suffer this injury, they would not be treated fairly and impartially. By protecting duties of various kinds, an unnatural quantity of capital is directed towards manufactures and commerce and taken from the land; and while, on account of these duties, they are obliged to purchase both homemade and foreign goods at a kind of monopoly price, they would be obliged to sell their own at the price of the most enlarged competition. It may fairly indeed be said, that to restore the freedom of the corn trade, while protecting duties on various other commodities are allowed to remain, is not really to restore things to their natural level, but to depress the cultivation of the land below other kinds of industry. And though, even in this case, it might still be a national advantage to purchase corn where it could be had the cheapest; yet it must be allowed that the owners of property in land would not be treated with impartial justice.

If under all the circumstances of the case, it should appear impolitic to check our agriculture; and so desirable to secure an independent supply of corn, as to justify the continued interference of the legislature for this purpose, the next question for our consideration is;

Fifthly, how far and by what sacrifices, restrictions upon the importation of foreign corn are calculated to attain the end in view.

With regard to the mere practicability of effecting an independent supply, it must certainly be allowed that foreign corn may be so prohibited as completely to secure this object. A country with a large territory, which determines never to import corn, except when the price indicates a scarcity, will unquestionably in average years supply its own wants. But a law passed with this view might be so framed as to effect its object rather by a diminution of the people than an increase of the corn: And even if constructed in the most judicious manner, it can never be made entirely free from objections of this kind.

The evils which must always belong to restrictions upon the importation of foreign corn, are the following:

1. A certain waste of the national resources, by the employment of a greater quantity of capital than is necessary for procuring the quantity of corn required.

2. A relative disadvantage in all foreign commercial transactions, occasioned by the high comparative prices of
   corn and labour, and the low value of silver, as far as
   they affect exportable commodities.

3. Some check to population, occasioned by a check to that
   abundance of corn, and demand for manufacturing labours, which would be the result of a perfect freedom of
   importation.

4. The necessity of constant revision and interference,
   which belongs to almost every artificial system.

It is true, that during the last twenty years we have witnessed a
very great increase of population and of our exported commodities,
under a high price of corn and labour; but this must have happened in
spite of these high prices, not in consequence of them; and is to be
attributed chiefly to the unusual success of our inventions for saving
labour and the unusual monopoly of the commerce of Europe which has
been thrown into our hands by the war. When these inventions spread
and Europe recovers in some degree her industry and capital, we may
not find it so easy to support the competition. The more strongly the
natural state of the country directs it to the purchase of foreign corn,
the higher must be the protecting duty or the price of importation, in
order to secure an independent supply; and the greater consequently
will be the relative disadvantage which we shall suffer in our commerce
with other countries. This drawback may, it is certain, ultimately be so
great as to counterbalance the effects of our extraordinary skill, capital
and machinery.

The whole, therefore, is evidently a question of contending advantages and disadvantages; and, as interests of the highest importance
are concerned, the most mature deliberation is required in its decision.

In whichever way it is settled, some sacrifices must be submitted
to. Those who contend for the unrestrained admission of foreign corn,
must not imagine that the cheapness it will occasion will be an unmixed
good; and that it will give an additional stimulus to the commerce and
population of the country, while it leaves the present state of agriculture and its future increase undisturbed. They must be prepared to
see a sudden stop put to the progress of our cultivation, and even some
diminution of its actual state; and they must be ready to encounter the

as yet untried risk, of making a considerable proportion of our population dependent upon foreign supplies of grain, and of exposing them to those vicissitudes and changes in the channels of commerce to which manufacturing states are of necessity subject.

On the other hand, those who contend for a continuance and increase of restrictions upon importation, must not imagine that the present state of agriculture and its present rate of eminence can be maintained without injuring other branches of the national industry. It is certain that they will not only be injured, but that they will be injured rather more than agriculture is benefited; and that a determination at all events to keep up the prices of our corn might involve us in a system of regulations, which, in the new state of Europe which is expected, might not only retard in some degree, as hitherto, the progress of our foreign commerce, but ultimately begin to diminish it; in which case our agriculture itself would soon suffer, in spite of all our efforts to prevent it.

If, on weighing fairly the good to be obtained and the sacrifices to be made for it, the legislature should determine to adhere to its present policy of restrictions, it should be observed, in reference to the mode of doing it, that the time chosen is by no means favourable for the adoption of such a system of regulations as will not need future alterations. The state of the currency must throw the most formidable obstacles in the way of all arrangements respecting the prices of importation.

If we return to cash payments, while bullion continues of its present value compared with corn, labour, and most other commodities; little alteration will be required in the existing corn laws. The bullion price of corn is now very considerably under sixty-three shillings, the price at which the high duty ceases according to the Act of 1804.

If our currency continues at its present nominal value, it will be necessary to make very considerable alterations in the laws, or they will be a mere dead letter and become entirely inefficient in restraining the importation of foreign corn.

If, on the other hand, we should return to our old standard, and at the same time the value of bullion should fall from the restoration of general confidence, and the ceasing of an extraordinary demand for bullion; an intermediate sort of alteration will be necessary, greater than in the case first mentioned, and less than in the second.

In this state of necessary uncertainty with regard to our currency, it would be extremely impolitic to come to any final regulation, founded on an average which would be essentially influenced by the nominal prices of the last five years.

To these considerations it may be added, that there are many reasons to expect a more than usual abundance of corn in Europe during the repose to which we may now look forward. Such an abundance[3] took place after the termination of the war of Louis XIV, and seems still more probable now, if the late devastation of the human race and interruption to industry should be succeeded by a peace of fifteen or twenty years.

The prospect of an abundance of this kind, may to some perhaps appear to justify still greater efforts to prevent the introduction of foreign corn; and to secure our agriculture from too sudden a shock, it may be necessary to give it some protection. But if, under such circumstances with regard to the price of corn in Europe, we were to endeavor to retain the prices of the last five years, it is scarcely possible to suppose that our foreign commerce would not in a short time begin to languish. The difference between ninety shillings a quarter and thirty-two shillings a quarter, which is said to be the price of the best wheat in France, is almost too great for our capital and machinery to contend with. The wages of labour in this country, though they have not risen in proportion to the price of corn, have been beyond all doubt considerably influenced by it.

If the whole of the difference in the expense of raising corn in this country and in the corn countries of Europe was occasioned by taxation, and the precise amount of that taxation as affecting corn, could be clearly ascertained; the simple and obvious way of restoring things to their natural level and enabling us to grow corn, as in a state of perfect freedom, would be to lay precisely the same amount of tax on imported corn and grant the same amount in a bounty upon exportation. Dr. Smith observes, that when the necessities of a state have obliged it to lay a tax upon a home commodity, a duty of equal amount upon the same kind of commodity when imported from abroad, only tends to restore the level of industry which had necessarily been disturbed by the tax.

But the fact is that the whole difference of price does not by any means arise solely from taxation. A part of it, and I should think, no inconsiderable part, is occasioned by the necessity of yearly cultivating and improving more poor land, to provide for the demands of an increasing population; which land must of course require more labour and dressing, and expense of all kinds in its cultivation. The growing price of corn therefore, independently of all taxation, is probably higher than in the rest of Europe; and this circumstance not only increases the sacrifice that must be made for an independent supply, but enhances the difficulty of framing a legislative provision to secure it.

When the former very high duties upon the importation of foreign grain were imposed, accompanied by the grant of a bounty, the growing price of corn in this country was not higher than in the rest of Europe; and the stimulus given to agriculture by these laws aided by other favourable circumstances occasioned so redundant a growth, that the average price of corn was not affected by the prices of importation. Almost the only sacrifice made in this case was the small rise of price occasioned by the bounty on its first establishment, which, after it had increased operated as a stimulus to cultivation, terminated in a period of cheapness.

If we were to attempt to pursue the same system in a very different state of the country, by raising the importation prices and the bounty in proportion to the fall in the value of money, the effects of the measure might bear very little resemblance to those which took place before. Since 1740 Great Britain has added nearly four millions and a half to her population, and with the addition of Ireland probably eight millions, a greater proportion I believe than in any other country in Europe; and from the structure of our society and the great increase of the middle classes, the demands for the products of pasture have probably been augmented in a still greater proportion. Under these circumstances it is scarcely conceivable that any effects could make us again export corn to the same comparative extent as in the middle of the last century. An increase of the bounty in proportion to the fall in the value of money, would certainly not be sufficient; and probably nothing could accomplish it but such an excessive premium upon exportation, as would at once stop the progress of the population and foreign commerce of the country, in order to let the produce of corn get before it.

In the present state of things then we must necessarily give up the idea of creating a large average surplus. And yet very high duties upon importation, operating alone, are peculiarly liable to occasion great fluctuations of price. It has been already stated, that after they have succeeded in producing an independent supply by steady high prices, an abundant crop which cannot be relieved by exportation, must occasion a very sudden fall.[4] Should this continue a second or third year, it would unquestionably discourage cultivation, and the country would again become partially dependent. The necessity of importing foreign corn would of course again raise the price of importation, and the same causes might make a similar fall and a subsequent rise recur; and thus prices would tend to vibrate between the high prices occasioned by the high duties on importation and the low prices occasioned by a glut which could not be relieved by exportation.

It is under these difficulties that the Parliament is called upon to legislate. On account of the deliberation which the subject naturally requires, but more particularly on account of the present uncertain state of the currency, it would be desirable to delay any final regulation. Should it however be determined to proceed immediately to a revision of the present laws, in order to render them more efficacious, there would be some obvious advantages, both as a temporary and perma-nent measure, in giving to the restrictions the form of a constant duty upon foreign corn, not to act as a prohibition, but as a protecting, and at the same time, profitable tax. And with a view to prevent the great fall that might be occasioned by a glut, under the circumstances before adverted to, but not to create an average surplus, the old bounty might be continued, and allowed to operate in the same way as the duty at all times, except in extreme cases.

These regulations would be extremely simple and obvious in their operations, would give greater certainty to the foreign grower, afford a profitable tax to the government, and would be less affected even by the expected improvement of the currency, than high importation prices founded upon any past average.[5]

Notes

1. From the reign of Edward III to the reign of Henry VII, a day's earnings, in corn, rose from a peck to near half a bushel, and from Henry VII to the end of Elizabeth, it fell from near half a bushel to little more than half a peck.

2. Wealth of Nations, b. iv, c. 2, p. 202.

3. The cheapness of corn, during the first half of the last century, was rather oddly mistaken by Dr. Smith for a rise in the value of silver. That it was owing to peculiar abundance was obvious, from all other commodities rising instead of falling.

4. The sudden fall of the price of corn this year seems to be a case precisely in point. It should be recollected, however, that quantity always in some degree balances cheapness.

5. Since sending the above to the press I have heard of the new resolutions that are to be proposed. The machinery seems to be a little complicated; but if it will work easily and well, they are greatly preferable to those which were suggested last year.

   To the free exportation asked, no rational objection can of course be made, though its efficiency in the present state of things may be doubted. With regard to the duties, if any be imposed, there must always be a question of degree. The principal objection which I see to the present scale, is that with an average price of corn in the actual state of the currency, there will be a pretty strong competition of foreign grain; whereas with an average price on the restoration of the currency, foreign competition will be absolutely and entirely excluded.

The Grounds of an Opinion on the Policy of Restricting the Importation of Foreign Corn; Intended as an Appendix to "Observations on the Corn Laws"

T.R. Malthus; 1815

The professed object of the *Observations on the Corn Laws*, which I published in the spring of 1814, was to state with the strictest impartiality the advantages and disadvantages which, in the actual circumstances of our present situation, were likely to attend the measures under consideration, respecting the trade in corn.

A fair review of both sides of the question, without any attempt to conceal the peculiar evils, whether temporary or permanent, which might belong to each, appeared to me of use, not only to assist in forming an enlightened decision on the subject, but particularly to prepare the public for the specific consequences which were to be expected from that decision, on whatever side it might be made. Such a preparation, from some quarter or other, seemed to be necessary, to prevent those just discontents which would naturally have arisen, if the measure adopted had been attended with results very different from those which had been promised by its advocates, or contemplated by the legislature.

With this object in view, it was neither necessary, nor desirable, that I should myself express a decided opinion on the subject. It would hardly, indeed, have been consistent with that character of impartiality, which I wished to give to my statements, and in which I have reason to believe I in some degree succeeded.[1]

These previous statements, however, having been given, and having, I hope, shown that the decision, whenever it is made, must be a compromise of contending advantages and disadvantages, I have no objection now to state (without the least reserve), and I can truly say, with the most complete freedom from all interested motives, the grounds of a deliberate, yet decided, opinion in favour of some restrictions on the importation of foreign corn.

This opinion has been formed, as I wished the readers of the *Observations* to form their opinions, by looking fairly at the difficulties on both sides of the question; and without vainly expecting to attain unmixed results, determining on which side there is the greatest balance of good with the least alloy of evil. The grounds on which the opinion so formed rests, are partly those which were stated in the *Observations*, and partly, and indeed mainly, some facts which have occurred during the last year, and which have given, as I think, a decisive weight to the side of restrictions. These additional facts are:

First, the evidence, which has been laid before Parliament, relating to the effects of the present prices of corn, together with the experience of the present year.

Secondly, the improved state of our exchanges, and the fall in the price of bullion.

Thirdly, and mainly, the actual laws respecting the exportation of corn lately passed in France.

1. In the *Observations on the Corn Laws*, I endeavored to show that, according to the general principles of supply and demand, a considerable fall in the price of corn could not take place, without throwing much poor lad out of cultivation, and effectually preventing, for a considerable time, all further improvements in agriculture, which have for their object an increase of produce.

The general principles, on which I calculated upon these consequences, have been fully confirmed by the evidence brought before the two houses of Parliament; and the effects of a considerable fall in the price of corn, and of the expected continuance of low prices, have shown themselves in a very severe shock to the cultivation of the country and a great loss of agricultural capital.

Whatever may be said of the peculiar interests and natural partialities of those who were called upon to give evidence upon this occasion, it is impossible not to be convinced, by the whole body of it taken together, that, during the last twenty years, and particularly during the last seven, there has been a great increase of capital laid out upon the land, and a great consequent extension of cultivation and improvement; that the system of spirited improvement and high farming, as it is technically called, has been principally encouraged by the progressive rise of prices owing in a considerable degree, to the difficulties thrown in the way of importation of foreign corn by the war; that the rapid accumulation of capital on the land, which it had occasioned, had so increased our home growth of corn, that, notwithstanding a great increase of population, we had become much less dependent upon foreign supplies for our support; and that the land was still deficient in capital, and would admit of the employment of such an addition to its present amount, as would be competent to the full supply of a greatly increased population: But that the fall of prices, which had lately taken place, and the alarm of a still further fall, from continued importation, had not only checked all progress of improvement, but had already occasioned a considerable loss of agricultural advances; and that a continuation of low prices would, in spite of a diminution of rents, unquestionably destroy a great mass of farming capital all over the country, and essentially diminish its cultivation and produce.

It has been sometimes said, that the losses at present sustained by farmers are merely the natural and necessary consequences of overtrading, and that they must bear them as all other merchants do, who have entered into unsuccessful speculations. But surely the question is not, or at least ought not to be, about the losses and profits of farmers, and the present condition of landholders compared with the past. It may be necessary, perhaps, to make inquiries of this kind, with a view to ulterior objects; but the real question respects the great loss of national wealth, attributed to a change in the spirit of our legislative enactments relating to the admission of foreign corn.

We have certainly no right to accuse our farmers of rash speculation for employing so large a capital in agriculture. The peace, it must be allowed, was most unexpected; and if the war had continued, the actual quantity of capital applied to the land, might have been as necessary to save the country from extreme want in future, as it obviously was in 1812, when, with the price of corn at above six guineas a quarter, we could only import a little more than one hundred thousand quarters. If, from the very great extension of cultivation, during the four or five preceding years, we had not obtained a very great increase of average produce, the distresses of that year would have assumed a most serious aspect.

There is certainly no one cause which can affect mercantile concerns, at all comparable in the extent of its effects, to the cause now operating upon agricultural capital. Individual losses must have the same distressing consequences in both cases, and they are often more complete, and the fall is greater, in the shocks of commerce. But I doubt, whether in the most extensive mercantile distress that ever took in this country, there was ever one fourth of the property, or one tenth of the number of individuals concerned, when compared with the effects of the present rapid fall of raw produce, combined with the very scanty crop of last year.[2]

Individual losses of course become national, according as they affect a greater mass of the national capital, and a greater number of individuals; and I think it must be allowed further, that no loss, in proportion to its amount, affects the interest of the nation so deeply, and vitally, and is so difficult to recover, as the loss of agricultural capital and produce.

If it be the intention of the legislature fairly to look at the evils, as well as the good, which belongs to both sides of the question, it must be allowed, that the evidence laid before the two houses of Parliament, and still more particularly the experience of the last year, show, that the immediate evils which are capable of being remedied by a system of restrictions, are of no inconsiderable magnitude.

2. In the *Observations on the Corn Laws*, I gave, as a reason for some delay in coming to a final regulation respecting the price at which foreign corn might be imported, the very uncertain state of the currency. I observed, that three different importation prices would be necessary, according as our currency should either rise to the then price of bullion, should continue at the same nominal value, or should take an intermediate position, founded on a fall in the value of bullion, owing to the discontinuance of an extraordinary demand for it, and a rise in the value of paper, owing to the prospect of a return to payments in specie. In the course of this last year, the state of our exchanges, and the fall in the price of bullion, show pretty clearly, that the intermediate alteration which, I then contemplated, greater than in the case first mentioned, and less than in the second, is the one which might be adopted with a fair prospect of permanence; and that we should not now proceed under the same uncertainty respecting the currency, which we should have done, if we had adopted a final regulation in the early part of last year.[3] This intermediate alteration, however, supposes a rise in the value of paper on a return to cash payments, and some general fall of prices quite unconnected with any regulations respecting the corn trade.[4]

But, if some fall of prices must take place from this cause, and if such a fall can never take place without a considerable check to industry, and discouragement to the accumulation of capital, it certainly does not seem a well-chosen time for the legislature to occasion another fall still greater, by departing at once from a system of restrictions which it had pursued with steadiness during the greatest part of the last century and, after having given up for a short period, had adopted again as its final policy in its two last enactments respecting the trade in corn. Even if it be intended. Finally, to throw open our ports, it might be wise to pass some temporary regulations, in order to prevent the very great shock which must take place, if the two causes here noticed, of the depreciation of commodities, be allowed to produce their full effect by contemporaneous action.

3. I stated, in the *Observations on the Corn Laws*, that the cheapness and steadiness in the price of corn, which were promised by the advocates of restrictions, were not attainable by the measures they proposed; that it was really impossible for us to grow at home a sufficiency for our own consumption, without keeping up the price of corn considerably above the average of the rest of Europe; and that, while this was the case, as we could never export to any advantage, we should always be liable to the variations of price, occasioned by the glut of a superabundant harvest; in short, that it must be allowed that a free trade in corn would, in all ordinary cases, not only secure a cheaper, but a more steady, supply of grain.

In expressing this distinct opinion on the effects of a free trade in corn, I certainly meant to refer to a trade really free—that is, a trade by which a nation would be entitled to its share of the produce of the commercial world, according to its means of purchasing, whether that produce were plentiful or scanty. In this sense I adhere strictly to the opinion I then gave; but, since that period, an event has occurred which has shown, in the clearest manner, that it is entirely out of our power, even in time of peace, to obtain a free trade in corn, or an approximation towards it, whatever may be our wishes on the subject.

It has, perhaps, not been sufficiently attended to in general, when the advantages of a free trade in corn have been discussed, that the jealousies and fears of nations, respecting their means of subsistence, will very rarely allow of a free egress of corn, when it is in any degree scarce. Our own statutes, till the very last year, prove these fears with regard to ourselves; and regulations of the same tendency occasionally come in aid of popular clamour in almost all countries of Europe. But the laws respecting the exportation of corn, which have been passed in France during the last year, have brought this subject home to us in the most striking and impressive manner. Our nearest neighbour, possessed of the largest and finest corn country in Europe, and who, owing to a more favourable climate and soil, a more stationary and comparatively less crowded population, and a lighter weight of taxation, can grow corn at less than half our prices, has enacted, that the exportation of corn shall be free till the price rises to about forty-nine shillings a quarter,[5] and that then it shall be entirely cease.[6]

From the vicinity of France, and the cheapness of its corn in all years of common abundance, it is scarcely possible that our main imports should not come from that quarter as long as our ports are open to receive them. In this first year of open trade, our imports have been such, as to show, that though the corn of the Baltic cannot seriously depress our prices in an unfavourable season at home, the corn of France may make it fall below a growing price, under the pressure of one of the worst crops that has been known for a long series of years.

I have at present before me an extract from a Rouen paper, containing the prices of corn in fourteen different markets for the first week in October, the average of which appears to be about thirty-eight shillings a quarter;[7] and this was after disturbances had taken place both at Havre and Dieppe, on account of the quantity exported, and the rise of prices which it had occasioned.

It may be said, perhaps, that the last harvest of France has been a very favourable one, and affords no just criterion of its general prices. But, from all that I hear, prices have often been as low during the last ten years. And, an average not exceeding forty shillings a quarter may, I think, be conclusively inferred from the price at which exportation is by law to cease.

At a time when, according to Adam Smith, the growing price in this country was only twenty-eight shillings a quarter, and the average price, including years of scarcity, only thirty-three shillings, exportation was not prohibited till the price rose to forty-eight shillings. It was the intention of the English government, at that time, to encourage agriculture by giving vent to its produce. We may presume that the same motive influenced the government of France in the late act respecting exportation. And it is fair therefore to conclude, that the price of wheat, in common years, is considerably less than the price at which exportation is to cease.

With these prices so near us, and with the consequent power of supplying ourselves with great comparative rapidity, which in the corn trade is a point of the greatest importance, there can be no doubt that, if our ports were open, our principal supplies of grain would come from France; and that, in all years of common plenty in that country, we should import more largely from it than from the Baltic. But from this quarter, which would then become our main and most habitual source of supply, all assistance would be at once cut off, in every season of only moderate scarcity; and we should have to look to other quarters, from which it is an established fact, that large sudden supplies cannot be obtained, not only for our usual imports, and the natural variations which belong to them, but for those which had been suddenly cut off from France, and which our habitually deficient growth had now rendered absolutely necessary.

To open our ports, under these circumstances, is not to obtain a free trade in corn; and, while I should say, without hesitation, that a free trade in corn was calculated to produce steadier prices than the system of restrictions with which it has been compared, I should, with as little hesitation say, that such a trade in corn, as has been described, would be subject to much more distressing and cruel variations, than the most determined system of prohibitions.

Such a species of commerce in grain shakes the foundations, and alters entirely the data on which the general principles of free trade are established. For what do these principles say? They say, and say most justly, that if every nation were to devote itself particularly to those kinds of industry and produce, to which its soil, climate, situation, capital, and skill, were best suited; and were then freely to exchange these products with each other, it would be the most certain and efficacious mode, not only of advancing the wealth and prosperity of the whole body of the commercial republic with the quickest pace, but of giving to each individual nation of the body the full and perfect use of all its resources.

I am very far indeed from meaning to insinuate, that if we cannot have the most perfect freedom of trade, we should have none; or that a great nation must immediately alter its commercial policy, whenever any of the countries with which it deals passes laws inconsistent with the principles of freedom. But I protest most entirely against the doctrine, that we are to pursue our general principles without ever looking to see if they are applicable to the case before us; and that in politics and political economy, we are to go straight forward, as we certainly ought to do in morals, without any reference to the conduct and proceedings of others.

There is no person in the least acquainted with political economy, but must be aware that the advantages resulting from the division of labour, as applicable to nations as well as individuals, depend solely and entirely on the power of exchanging subsequently the products of labour. And no one can hesitate to allow, that it is completely in the power of others to prevent such exchanges, and to destroy entirely the advantages which would otherwise result from the application of individual or national industry, to peculiar and appropriate products.

Let us suppose, for instance, that the inhabitants of the Lowlands of Scotland were to say to the Highlanders, 'We will exchange our corn for your cattle, whenever we have a superfluity; but if our crops in any degree fail, you must not expect to have a single grain': Would not the question respecting the policy of the present change, which is taking place in the Highlands, rest entirely upon different grounds? Would it not be perfectly senseless in the Highlanders to think only of those general principles which direct them to employ the soil in the way that is best suited to it? If supplies of corn could not be obtained with some degree of steadiness and certainty from other quarters, would it not be absolutely necessary for them to grow it themselves, however ill adapted to it might be their soil and climate?

The same may be said of all the pasture districts of Great Britain, compared with the surrounding corn countries. If they could only obtain the superfluities of their neighbours, and were entitled to no share of the produce when it was scarce, they could not certainly devote themselves with any degree of safety to their present occupations.

There is, on this account, a grand difference between the freedom of the home trade in corn, and the freedom of the foreign trade. A government of tolerable vigour can make the home trade in corn really free. It can secure to the pasture districts, or the towns that must be fed from a distance, their share of the general produce, whether plentiful or scarce. It can set them quite at rest about the power of exchanging the peculiar products of their own labour for the other products which are necessary to them, and can dispense, therefore, to all its subjects, the inestimable advantages of an unrestricted intercourse.

But it is not in the power of any single nation to secure the freedom of the foreign trade in corn. To accomplish this, the concurrence of many others is necessary; and this concurrence, the fears and jealousies so universally prevalent about the means of subsistence, almost invariably prevent. There is hardly a nation in Europe which does not occasionally exercise the power of stopping entirely, or heavily taxing, its exports of grain, if prohibitions do not form part of its general code of laws.

The question then before us is evidently a special, not a general one. It is not a question between the advantages of a free trade, and a system of restrictions; but between a specific system of restrictions formed by ourselves for the purpose of rendering us, in average years, nearly independent of foreign supplies, and the specific system of restricted importations, which alone it is in our power to obtain under the existing laws of France, and in the actual state of the other countries of the continent.[8]

In looking, in the first place, at the resources of the country, with a view to an independent supply for an increasing population; and comparing subsequently the advantages of the two systems abovementioned, without overlooking their disadvantages, I have fully made up my mind as to the side on which the balance lies; and am decidedly of opinion, that a system of restrictions so calculated as to keep us, in average years, nearly independent of foreign supplies of corn, will more effectually conduce to the wealth and prosperity of the country, and of by far the greatest mass of the inhabitants, than the opening of our ports for the free admission of foreign corn, in the actual state of Europe.

Of the resources of Great Britain and Ireland for the further growth of corn, by the further application of capital to the land, the evidence laid before Parliament furnishes the most ample testimony. But it is not necessary, for this purpose, to recur to evidence that may be considered as partial. All the most intelligent works which have been written on agricultural subjects of late years, agree in the same statements; and they are confirmed beyond a possibility of doubt, when we consider the extraordinary improvements, and prodigious increase of produce that have taken place latterly in some districts, which, in point of natural soil, are not superior to others that are still yielding the most scanty and miserable crops. Most of the light soils of the kingdom might, with adequate capital and skill, be made to equal the improved parts of Norfolk; and the vast tracts of clay lands that are yet in a degraded state almost all over the kingdom, are susceptible of a degree of improvement, which it is by no means easy to fix, but which certainly offers a great prospective increase of produce. There is even a chance (but on this I will not insist) of a diminution in the real price of corn,[9] owing to the extension of those great improvements, and that great economy and good management of labour, of which we have such intelligent accounts from Scotland.[10] If these clay lands, by draining, and the plentiful application of lime and other manures, could be so far meliorated in quality as to admit of being worked by two horses and a single man, instead of three or four horses with a man and a boy, what a vast saving of labour and expense would at once be effected, at the same time that the crops would be prodigiously increased! And such an improvement may rationally be expected, from what has really been accomplished in particular districts. In short, if merely the best modes of cultivation, now in use in some parts of Great Britain, were generally extended, and the whole country was brought to a level, in proportion to its natural advantages of soil and situation, by the further accumulation and more equable distribution of capital and skill; the quantity of additional produce would be immense, and would afford the means of subsistence to a very great increase of population.

In some countries possessed of a small territory, and consisting perhaps chiefly of one or two large cities, it never can be made a question, whether or not they should freely import foreign corn. They exist, in fact, by this importation; and being always, in point of population, inconsiderable, they may, in general, rely upon a pretty regular supply. But whether regular or not, they have no choice. Nature has clearly told them, that if they increase in wealth and power to any extent, it can only be by living upon the raw produce of other countries.

It is quite evident that the same alternative is not presented to Great Britain and Ireland, and that the united empire has ample means of increasing in wealth, population, and power, for a very long course of years, without being habitually dependent upon foreign supplies for the means of supporting its inhabitants.

As we have clearly, therefore, our choice between two systems, under either of which we may certainly look forwards to a progressive increase of population and power; it remains for us to consider in which way the greatest portion of wealth and happiness may be steadily secured to the largest mass of the people.

1. And first let us look to the labouring classes of society, as the foundation on which the whole fabric rests; and, from their numbers, unquestionably of the greatest weight, in any estimate of national happiness.

If I were convinced, that to open our ports, would be permanently to improve the condition of the labouring classes of society, I should consider the question as at once determined in favour of such a measure. But I own it appears to me, after the most deliberate attention to the subject, that it will be attended with effects very different from those of improvement. We are very apt to be deceived by names, and to be captivated with the idea of cheapness, without reflecting that the term is merely relative, and that it is very possible for a people to be miserably poor, and some of them starving, in a country where the money price of corn is very low. Of this the histories of Europe and Asia will afford abundant instances.

In considering the condition of the lower classes of society, we must consider only the real exchangeable value of labour; that is, its power of commanding the necessaries, conveniences, and luxuries of life.

I stated in the *Observations*, and more at large in the *Inquiry into Rents*,[11] that under the same demand for labour, and the same consequent power of purchasing the means of subsistence, a high money price of corn would give the labourer a very great advantage in the purchase of the conveniences and luxuries of life. The effect of this high money price would not, of course, be so marked among the very poorest of the society, and those who had the largest families; because so very great a part of their earnings must be employed in absolute necessaries. But to all those above the very poorest, the advantage of wages resulting from a price of eighty shillings a quarter for wheat, compared with fifty or sixty, would in the purchase of tea, sugar, cotton, linens, soap, candles, and many other articles, be such as to make their condition decidedly superior.

Nothing could counterbalance this, but a much greater demand for labour; and such an increased demand, in consequence of the opening of our ports, is at best problematical. The check to cultivation has been so sudden and decisive, as already to throw a great number of agricultural labourers out of employment;[12] and in Ireland this effect has taken place to such a degree, as to threaten the most distressing, and even alarming, consequences. The farmers, in some districts, have entirely lost the little capital they possessed; and, unable to continue in their farms, have deserted them, and left their labourers without the means of employment. In a country, the peculiar defects of which were already a deficiency of capital, and a redundancy of population, such a check to the means of employing labour must be attended with no common distress. In Ireland, it is quite certain, that there are no mercantile capitals ready to take up those persons who are thus thrown out of work, and even in Great Britain the transfer will be slow and difficult.

Our commerce and manufactures, therefore, must increase very considerably before they can restore the demand for labour already lost; for the and a moderate increase beyond this will scarcely make up disadvantage of a low money price of wages.

These wages will finally be determined by the usual money price of corn, and the state of the demand for labour.

There is a difference between what may be called the usual price of corn and the average price, which has not been sufficiently attended to. Let us suppose the common price of corn, for four years out of five, to be about £2 a quarter, and during the fifth year to be £6. The average price of the five years will then be £2 16s.; but the usual price will still be about £2, and it is by this price, and not by the price of a year of scarcity, or even the average including it, that wages are generally regulated.

If the ports were open, the usual price of corn would certainly fall, and probably the average price; but from at has before been said of the existing laws of France, and of the practice among the Baltic nations of raising the tax on their exported corn in proportion to the demand for it, there is every reason to believe, that the fluctuations of price would be much greater. Such would, at least, be my conclusion from theory; and, I think, it has been confirmed by the experience of the last hundred years. During this time, the period of our greatest importations, and of our greatest dependence upon foreign corn, was from 1792 to 1805 inclusive; and certainly in no fourteen years of the whole hundred were the fluctuations of price so great. In 1792 the price was 42s. a quarter; in 1796, 77s.; in 1801, 118s. a quarter; and, in 1803, 56s. Between the year 1792 and 1801 the rise was almost a triple, and in the short period from 1798 to 1803, it rose from 50s. to 118s. and fell again to 56s.[13]

I would not insist upon this existence as absolutely conclusive, on account of the mixture of accident in all such appeals to facts; but it certainly tends to confirm the probability of those great fluctuations which, according to all general principles, I should expect from the temper and customs of nations, with regard to the egress of corn, when it is scarce; and particularly from the existing laws of that country, which, in all common years, will furnish us with a large proportion of our supplies.

To these causes of temporary fluctuations, during peace, should be added the more durable as well as temporary, fluctuations occasioned by war. Without reference to the danger of excessive scarcity from another combination against us, if we are merely driven back at certain distant intervals upon our own resources, the experience of the present times will teach us not to estimate lightly the convulsion which attends the return, and the evils of such alternations of price.

In the *Observations*, I mentioned some causes of fluctuations which would attend the system of restrictions; but they are in my opinion inconsiderable, compared with those which have been just referred to.

On the labouring classes, therefore, the effects of opening our ports for the free importation of foreign corn, will be greatly to lower their wages, and to subject them to much greater fluctuations of price. And, in this state of things, it will require a much greater increase in the demand for labour, than there is in any rational ground for expecting, to compensate to the labourer the advantages which he loses in the high money wages of labour, and the steadier and less fluctuating price of corn.

2. Of the next most important class of society, those who live upon the profits of stock, one half probably are farmers, or immediately connected with farmers; and of the property of the other half, not above one fourth is engaged in foreign trade.

Of the farmers it is needless to say anything. It cannot be doubted that they will suffer severely from the opening of the ports. Not that the profits of farming will not recover themselves, after a certain period, and be as great, or perhaps greater, than they were before; but this cannot take place till after a great loss of agricultural capital, or the removal of it into the channels of commerce and manufactures.

Of the commercial and manufacturing part of the society, only those who are directly engaged in foreign trade, will feel the benefit of the importing system. It is of course to be expected, that the foreign trade of the nation will increase considerably. If it do not, indeed, we shall have experienced a very severe loss, without anything like a compensation for it. And if this increase merely equals the loss of produce sustained by agriculture, the quantity of other produce remaining the same, it is quite clear that the country cannot possibly gain by the exchange, at whatever price it may buy or sell. Wealth does not consist in the dearness or cheapness of the usual measure of value, but in the quantity of produce; and to increase effectively this quantity of produce, after the severe check sustained by agriculture, it is necessary that commerce should make a very powerful start.

In the actual state of Europe and the prevailing jealousy of our manufactures, such a start seems quite doubtful; and it is by no means impossible that we shall be obliged to pay for our foreign corn, by importing less of other commodities, as well as by exporting more of our manufactures.

It may be said, perhaps, that a fall in the price of our corn and labour, affords the only chance to our manufacturers of retaining possession of the foreign markets; and that though the produce of the country may not be increased by the fall in the price of corn, such a fall is necessary to prevent a positive diminution of it. There is some weight undoubtedly in this argument. But if we look at the probable effects of returning peace to Europe, it is impossible to suppose that, even with a considerable diminution in the price of labour, we should not lose some markets on the continent, for those manufactures in which we have no peculiar advantage; while we have every reason to believe that in others, where our colonies, our navigation, our long credits, our coals, and our mines come in question, as well as our skill and capital, we shall retain our trade in spite of high wages. Under these circumstances, it seems peculiarly advisable to maintain unimpaired, if possible, the home market, and not to lose the demand occasioned by so much of the rents of land, and of the profits and capital of farmers, as must necessarily be destroyed by the check to our home produce.

But in whatever way the country may be affected by the change, we must suppose that those who are immediately engaged in foreign trade will benefit by it. As those, however, form but a very small portion of the class of persons living on the profits of stock, in point of number, and not probably above a seventh or eighth in point of property, their interests cannot be allowed to weigh against the interests of so very large a majority.

With regard to this great majority, it is impossible that they should not feel very widely and severely the diminution of their nominal capital by the fall of prices. We know the magic effect upon industry of a rise of prices. It has been noticed by Hume, and witnessed by every person who has attended to subjects of this kind. And the effects of a fall are proportionately depressing. Even the foreign trade will not escape its influence, though here it may be counterbalanced by a real increase of demand. But, in the internal trade, not only will the full effect of this deadening weight be experienced, but there is reason to fear that it may be accompanied with an actual diminution of home demand. There may be the same or even a greater quantity of corn consumed in the country, but a smaller quantity of manufactures and colonial produce; and our foreign corn may be purchased in part by commodities which were before consumed at home. In this case, the whole of the internal trade must severely suffer, and the wealth and enjoyments of the country be decidedly diminished. The quantity of a country's exports is a very uncertain criterion of its wealth. The quantity of produce permanently consumed at home is, perhaps, the most certain criterion of wealth to which we can refer.

Already, in all the country towns, this diminution of demand has been felt in a very great degree; and the surrounding farmers, who chiefly support them, are quite unable to make their accustomed purchases. If the home produce of grain be considerably diminished by the opening of our ports, of which there can be no doubt, these effects in the agricultural countries must be permanent, though not to the same extent as at present. And even if the manufacturing towns should ultimately increase, in proportion to the losses of the country, of which there is great reason to doubt, the transfer of wealth and population will be slow, painful, and unfavourable to happiness.

3. Of the class of landholders, it may be truly said, that though they do not so actively contribute to the production of wealth, as either of the classes just noticed, there is no class in society whose interests are more nearly and intimately connected with the prosperity of the state.

Some persons have been of opinion, and Adam Smith himself among others, that a rise or fall of the price of corn does not really affect the interests of the landholders; but both theory and experience prove the contrary; and show, that, under all common circumstances, a fall of price must be attended with a diminution of produce, and that a diminution of produce will naturally be attended with a diminution of rent.[14]

Of the effect, therefore, of opening the ports, in diminishing both the real and nominal rents of the landlords, there can be no doubt; and we must not imagine that the interest of a body of men, so circumstanced as the landlords, can materially suffer without affecting the interests of the state.

It has been justly observed by Adam Smith, that 'no equal quantity of productive labour employed in manufactures can ever occasion so great a reproduction as in agriculture.' If we suppose the rents of land taken throughout the kingdom to be one fourth of the gross produce, it is evident, that to purchase the same value of raw produce by means of manufactures, would require one third more capital. Every five thousand pounds laid out on the land, not only repays the usual profits of stock, but generates an additional value, which goes to the landlord.

And this additional value is not a mere benefit to a particular individual, or set of individuals, but affords the most steady home demand for the manufactures of the country, the most effective fund for its financial support, and the largest disposable force for its army and navy. It is true, that the last additions to the agricultural produce of an improving country are not attended with a large proportion of rent;[15] and it is precisely this circumstance that may make it answer to a rich country to import some of its corn, if it can be secure of obtaining an equable supply. But in all cases the importation of foreign corn must fail to answer nationally, if it is not so much cheaper than the corn that can be grown at home, as to equal both the profits and the rent of the grain which it displaces.

If two capitals of ten thousand pounds each, be employed, one in manufactures, and the other in the improvement of the land, with the usual profits, and withdrawn in twenty years, the one employed in manufactures will leave nothing behind it, while the one employed on the land will probably leave a rent of no inconsiderable value.

These considerations, which are not often attended to, if they do not affect the ordinary question of a free trade in corn, must at least be allowed to have weight, when the policy of such a trade is, from peculiarity of situation and circumstances, rendered doubtful.

4. We now come to a class of society, who will unquestionably be benefited by the opening of our ports. These are the stockholders, and those who live upon fixed salaries.[16] They are not only, however, small in number, compared with those who will be affected in a different manner; but their interests are not so closely interwoven with the welfare of the state, as the classes already considered, particularly the labouring classes, and the landlords.

In the *Observations*, I remarked, that it was an error of the most serious magnitude to suppose that any natural or artificial causes, which should raise or lower the values of corn or silver, might be considered as matters of indifference; and that, practically, no material change could take place in the value of either, without producing both temporary and lasting effects, which have a most powerful influence on the distribution of property.

In fact, it is perfectly impossible to suppose that, in any change in the measure of value, which ever did, or ever can take place practically, all articles, both foreign and domestic, and all incomes, from whatever source derived, should arrange themselves precisely in the same relative proportions as before. And if they do not, it is quite obvious, that such a change may occasion the most marked differences in the command possessed by individuals and classes of individuals over the produce and wealth of the country. Sometimes the changes of this kind that actually take place, are favourable to the industrious classes of society, and sometimes unfavourable.

It can scarcely be doubted, that one of the main causes, which has enabled us hitherto to support, with almost undiminished resources, the prodigious weight of debt which has been accumulated during the last twenty years, is the continued depreciation of the measure in which it has been estimated, and the great stimulus to industry, and power of accumulation, which have been given to the industrious classes of society by the progressive rise of prices. As far as this was occasioned by excessive issues of paper, the stockholder was unjustly treated, and the industrious classes of society benefited unfairly at his expense. But, on the other hand, if the price of corn were now to fall to fifty shillings a quarter, and labour and other commodities nearly in proportion, there can be no doubt that the stockholder would be benefited unfairly at the expense of the industrious classes of society, and consequently at the expense of the wealth and prosperity of the whole country.

During the twenty years, beginning with 1794 and ending with 1813, the average price of British corn per quarter was about eighty-three shillings; during the ten years ending with 1813, ninety-two shillings; and during the last five years of the twenty, one hundred and eight shillings. In the course of these twenty years, the government borrowed near five hundred millions of real capital, for which on a rough average, exclusive of the sinking fund, it engaged to pay about five per cent. But if corn should fall to fifty shillings a quarter, and other commodities in proportion, instead of an interest of about five per cent. the government would really pay an interest of seven, eight, nine, and for the last two hundred millions, ten per cent.

To this extraordinary generosity towards the stockholders, I should be disposed to make no kind of objection, if it were not necessary to consider by whom it is to be paid; and a moment's reflection will show us, that it can only be paid by the industrious classes of society and the landlords, that is, by all those whose nominal incomes will vary with the variations in the measure of value. The nominal revenues of this part of the society, compared with the average of the last five years, will be diminished one half; and out of this nominally reduced income, they will have to pay the same nominal amount of taxation.

The interest and charges of the national debt, including the sinking fund, are now little short of £40 millions a year; and these £40 millions, if we completely succeed in the reduction of the price of corn and labour, are to be paid in future from a revenue of about half the nominal value of the national income in 1813.

If we consider, with what an increased weight the taxes on tea, sugar, malt, leather, soap, candles, etc., would in this case bear on the labouring classes of society, and what proportion of their incomes all the active, industrious middle orders of the state, as well as the higher orders, must pay in assessed taxes, and the various articles of the customs and excise, the pressure will appear to be absolutely intolerable. Nor would even the ad valorem taxes afford any real relief. The annual £40 millions, must at all events be paid; and if some taxes fail, others must be imposed that will be more productive.

These are considerations sufficient to alarm even the stockholders themselves, indeed, if the measure of value were really to fall, as we have supposed, there is great reason to fear that the country would be absolutely unable to continue the payment of the present interest of the national debt.

I certainly do not think, that by opening our ports to the freest admission of foreign corn, we shall lower the price to fifty shillings a quarter. I have already given my reasons for believing that the fluctuations which in the present state of Europe, a system of importation would bring with it, would be often producing dear years, and throwing us back again upon our internal resources. But still there is no doubt whatever, that a free influx of foreign grain would in all commonly favourable seasons very much lower its price.

Let us suppose it lowered to sixty shillings a quarter, which for periods of three or four years together is not improbable. The difference between a measure of value at sixty compared with eighty (the price at which it is proposed to fix the importation), is thirty-three and one third per cent. This per cent upon £40 millions amounts to a very formidable sum. But let us suppose that corn does not effectually regulate the prices of other commodities; and, making allowances on this account, let us take only twenty-five, or even twenty per cent. Twenty per cent upon £40 millions amounts at once to £8 millions—a sum which ought to go a considerable way towards a peace establishment; but which, in the present case, must go to pay the additional interest of the national debt, occasioned by the change in the measure of value. And even if the price of corn be kept up by restrictions to eight shillings a quarter, it is certain that the whole of the loans made during the war just terminated, will on an average, be paid at an interest very much higher than they were contracted for; which increased interest can, of course, only be furnished by the industrious classes of society.

I own it appears to me that the necessary effect of a change in the measure of value on the weight of a large national debt is alone sufficient to make the question fundamentally different from that of a simple question about a free or restricted trade; and, that to consider it merely in this light, and to draw our conclusions accordingly, is to expect the same results from premises which have essentially changed their nature. From this review of the manner in which the different classes of society will be affected by the opening of our ports, I think it appears clearly, that very much the largest mass of the people, and particularly of the industrious orders of the state, will be more injured than benefited by the measure.

I have now stated the grounds on which it appears to me to be wise and politic, in the actual circumstances of the country, to restrain the free importation of foreign corn.

To put some stop to the progressive loss of agricultural capital, which is now taking place, and which it will be by no means easy to recover, it might be advisable to pass a temporary act of restriction, whatever may be the intention of the legislature in future. But, certainly it is much to be wished that as soon as possible, consistently with due deliberation, the permanent policy intended to be adopted with regard to the trade in corn should be finally settled. Already, in the course of little more than a century, three distinct changes in this policy have taken place. The act of William, which gave the bounty, combined with the prohibitory act of Charles II was founded obviously and strikingly upon the principle of encouraging exportation and discouraging importation; the spirit of the regulations adopted in 1773, and acted upon some time before, was nearly the reverse, and encouraged importation and discouraged exportation. Subsequently, as if alarmed at the dependence of the country upon foreign corn, and the fluctuations of price which it had occasioned, the legislature in a feeble act of 1791, and rather a more effective one in 1804, returned again to the policy of restrictions. And if the act of 1804 be left now unaltered, it may be fairly said that a fourth change has taken place; as it is quite certain that, to proceed consistently upon a restrictive system, fresh regulations become absolutely necessary to keep pace with the progressive fall in the value of currency.

Such changes in the spirit of our legislative enactments are much to be deprecated; and with a view to a greater degree of steadiness in future, it is quite necessary that we should be so fully prepared for the consequences which belong to each system, as not to have our determinations shaken by them, when they occur.

If, upon mature deliberation, we determine to open our ports to the free admission of foreign grain, we must not be disturbed at the depressed state, and diminished produce of our home cultivation; we must not be disturbed at our becoming more and more dependent upon other nations for the main support of our population; we must not be disturbed at the greatly increased pressure of the national debt upon the national industry; and we must not be disturbed at the fluctuations of price, occasioned by the very variable supplies, which we shall necessarily receive from France, in the actual state of her laws, or by the difficulty and expense of procuring large, and sudden imports from the Baltic, when our wants are pressing. These consequences may all be distinctly foreseen. Upon all general principles, they belong to the opening of our ports, in the actual state and relations of this country to the other countries of Europe; and though they may be counterbalanced or more than counterbalanced, by other advantages, they cannot, in the nature of things, be avoided.

On the other hand, if, on mature deliberation, we determine steadily to pursue a system of restrictions with regard to the trade in corn, we must not be disturbed at a progressive rise in the price of grain; we must not be disturbed at the necessity of altering, at certain intervals, our restrictive laws according to the state of the currency, and the value of the precious metals; we must not be disturbed at the progressive diminution of fixed incomes; and we must not be disturbed at the occasional loss or diminution of a continental market for some of our least peculiar manufactures, owing to the high price of our labour.[17] All these disadvantages may be distinctly foreseen. According to all general principles they strictly belong to the system adopted; and, though they may be counterbalanced, and more than counterbalanced, by other greater advantages, they cannot, in the nature of things, be avoided, if we continue to increase in wealth and population.

Those who promise low prices upon the restrictive system, take an erroneous view of the causes which determine the prices of raw produce, and draw an incorrect inference from the experience of the first half of the last century. As I have stated in another place,[18] a nation which vary greatly gets the start of its neighbours in riches, without any peculiar natural facilities for growing corn, must necessarily submit to one of these alternatives—either a very high comparative price of grain, or a very great dependence upon other countries for it.

With regard to the specific mode of regulating the importation of corn, if the restrictive system be adopted, I am not sufficiently acquainted with the details of the subject to be able to speak with confidence. It seems to be generally agreed, that, in the actual state of things, a price of about eighty shillings a quarter[19] would prevent our cultivation from falling back, and perhaps allow it to be progressive. But, in future, we should endeavor, if possible, to avoid all discussions about the necessity of protecting the British farmer, and securing to him a fair living profit. Such language may perhaps be allowable in a crisis like the present. But certainly the legislature has nothing to do with securing to any classes of its subjects a particular rate of profits in their different trades. This is not the province of a government; and it is unfortunate that any language should be used which may convey such an impression, and make people believe that their rulers ought to listen to the accounts of their gains and losses.

But a government may certainly see sufficient reasons for wishing to secure an independent supply of grain. This is a definite, and may be a desirable, object, of the same nature as the Navigation Act; and it is much to be wished, that this object, and not the interests of farmers and landlords, should be the ostensible, as well as the real, end which we have in view, in all our inquiries and proceedings relating to the trade in corn.

I firmly believe that, in the actual state of Europe, and under the actual circumstances of our present situation, it is our wisest policy to grow our own average supply of corn; and, in so doing, I feel persuaded that the country has ample resources for a great and continued increase of population, of power, of wealth, and of happiness.

Notes

1. Some of my friends were of different opinions as to the side, towards which my arguments most inclined. This I consider as a tolerably fair proof of impartiality.

2. Mercantile losses are always comparatively partial; but the present losses, occasioned by the unusual combination of low prices, and scanty produce, must inflict a severe blow upon the whole mass of cultivators. There never, perhaps, was known a year more injurious to the interests of agriculture.

3. At the same time, I certainly now very much wish that some regulation had been adopted last year. It would have saved the nation a great loss of agricultural capital, which it will take some time to recover. But it was impossible to foresee such a year as the present—such a combination, as a very bad harvest, and very low prices.

4. I have very little doubt that the value of paper in this country has already risen, notwithstanding the increased issues of the Bank. These increased issues I attribute chiefly to the great failures which have taken place among country banks, and the very great purchases which have been made for the continental markets, and, under these circumstances, increased issues might take place, accompanied even by a rise of value. But the currency has not yet recovered itself. The real exchange, during the last year, must have been greatly in our favour, although the nominal exchange is considerably against us. This shows, incontrovertibly, that our currency is still depreciated, in reference to the bullion currencies of the continent. A part, however, of this depreciation may still be owing to the value of bullion in Europe not having yet fallen to its former level.

5. Calculated at twenty-four livres the pound sterling.

6. It has been supposed by some, that this law cannot, and will not be executed; but, I own, I see no grounds for such an opinion. It is difficult to execute prohibitions against the exportation of corn, when it is in great plenty, but not when it is scarce. For ten years before 1757, we had in this country, regularly exported on an average,

above four hundred thousand quarters of wheat, and in that year there was at once an excess of importation. With regard to the alleged impotence of governments in this respect, it appears to me that facts show their power rather than their weakness. To be convinced of this, it is only necessary to look at the diminished importations from America during the war, and particularly from the Baltic after Bonaparte's decrees. The imports from France and the Baltic in 1810, were by special licenses, granted for purposes of revenue. Such licenses showed strength rather than weakness; and might have been refused, if a greater object than revenue had at that time presented itself.

7. The average is sixteen francs, twenty-one centimes, the hectolitre. The hectolitre is about one-twentieth less than three Winchester bushels, which makes the English quarter come to about thirty-eight shillings.

8. It appears from the evidence, that the corn from the Baltic is often very heavily taxed, and that this tax is generally raised in proportion to our necessities. In a scarce year in this country we could never get any considerable quantity of corn from the Baltic, without paying an enormous price for it.

9. By the real growing price of corn, I mean the real quantity of labour and capital which has been employed to procure the last additions which have been made to the national produce. In every rich and improving country there is a natural and strong tendency to a constantly increasing price of raw produce, owing to the necessity of employing, progressively, land of an inferior quality. But this tendency may be partially counteracted by great improvements in cultivation, and economy of labour. See this subject treated in *Inquiry into the Nature and Progress of Rent*, just published.

10. Sir John Sinclair's *Account of the Husbandry of Scotland*, and *General Report of Scotland*.

11. *Inquiry into the Nature and Progress of Rent*

12. I was not prepared to expect (as I intimated in the *Observations*) so sudden a fall in the price of labour as has already taken place. This

fall has been occasioned, not so much by the low price of corn, as by the sudden stagnation of agricultural work, occasioned by a more sudden check to cultivation than I foresaw.

13. I am strongly disposed to believe, that it is owing to the unwillingness of governments to allow the free egress of their corn, when it is scarce, that nations are practically so little dependent upon each other for corn, as they are found to be. According to all general principles they ought to be more dependent. But the great fluctuations in the price of corn, occasioned by this unwillingness, tend to throw each country back again upon its internal resources. This was remarkably the case with us in 1800 and 1801, when the very high price, which we paid for foreign corn, gave a prodigious stimulus to our domestic agriculture. A large territorial country, that imports foreign corn, is exposed not infrequently to the fluctuations which belong to this kind of variable dependence, without obtaining the cheapness that ought to accompany a trade in corn really free.

14. See this subject treated in *Inquiry into the Nature and Progress of Rent*.

15. *Inquiry into the Nature and Progress of Rent*

16. It is to this class of persons that I consider myself as chiefly belonging. Much the greatest part of my income is derived from a fixed salary and the interest of money in the funds.

17. It often happens that the high prices of a particular country may diminish the quantity of its exports without diminishing the value of their amount abroad; in which case its foreign trade is peculiarly advantageous, as it purchases the same amount of foreign commodities at a much less expense of labour and capital.

18. *Inquiry into the Nature and Progress of Rent*

19. This price seems to be pretty fairly consistent with the idea of getting rid of that part of our high prices which belongs to excessive issues of paper, and retaining only that part which belongs to great wealth, combined with a system of restrictions.

The High Price of Bullion,
A Proof of the Depreciation of Bank Notes

David Ricardo; 1810

The precious metals employed for circulating the commodities of the world, previously to the establishment of banks, have been supposed by the most approved writers on political economy to have been divided into certain proportions among the different civilized nations of the earth, according to the state of their commerce and wealth, and therefore according to the number and frequency of the payments which they had to perform. While so divided they preserved every where the same value, and as each country had an equal necessity for the quantity actually in use, there could be no temptation offered to either for their importation or exportation.

Gold and silver, like other commodities, have an intrinsic value, which is not arbitrary, but is dependent on their scarcity, the quantity of labour bestowed in procuring them, and the value of the capital employed in the mines which produce them.

"The quality of utility, beauty, and scarcity," says Dr. Smith, "are the original foundation of the high price of those metals, or of the great quantity of other goods for which they can every where be exchanged. This value was antecedent to, and independent of, their being employed as coin, and was the quality which fitted them for that employment."

If the quantity of gold and silver in the world employed as money were exceedingly small, or abundantly great, it would not in the least affect the proportions in which they would be divided among the different nations—the variation in their quantity would have produced no other effect than to make the commodities for which they were exchanged comparatively dear or cheap. The smaller quantity of money would perform the functions of a circulating medium, as well as the larger. Ten millions would be as effectual for that purpose as one hundred millions. Dr. Smith observes, "that the most abundant mines of the precious metals would add little to the wealth of the world. A produce of which the value is principally derived from its scarcity is necessarily degraded by its abundance."

If in the progress towards wealth, one nation advanced more rapidly than the others, that nation would require and obtain a greater proportion of the money of the world. Its commerce, its commodities, and its payments, would increase, and the general currency of the world would be divided according to the new proportions. All countries, therefore, would contribute their share to this effectual demand.

In the same manner, if any nation wasted part of its wealth, or lost part of its trade, it could not retain the same quantity of circulating medium which it before possessed. A part would be exported, and divided among the other nations till the usual proportions were reestablished.

While the relative situation of countries continued unaltered, they might have abundant commerce with each other, but their exports and imports would on the whole be equal. England might possibly import more goods from, than she would export to, France, but she would in consequence export more to some other country, and France would import more from that country; so that the exports and imports of all countries would balance each other; bills of exchange would make the necessary payments, but no money would pass because it would have the same value in all countries.

If a mine of gold were discovered in either of these countries, the currency of that country would be lowered in value in consequence of the increased quantity of the precious metals brought into circulation, and would therefore no longer be of the same value as that of other countries. Gold and silver, whether in coin or in bullion, obeying the law which regulates all other commodities, would immediately become articles of exportation; they would leave the country where they were cheap, for those countries where they were dear, and would continue to do so as long as the mine should prove productive, and till the proportion existing between capital and money in each country before the discovery of the mine, were again established, and gold and silver restored every where to one value. In return for the gold exported, commodities would be imported; and though what is usually termed the balance of trade would be against the country exporting money or bullion, it would be evident that she was carrying on a most advantageous trade, exporting that which was no way useful to her, for commodities which might be employed in the extension of her manufactures, and the increase of her wealth.

If instead of a mine being discovered in any country, a bank were established, such as the Bank of England, with the power of issuing its notes for a circulating medium; after a large amount had been issued, either by way of loan to merchants, or by advances to government, thereby adding considerably to the sum of the currency, the same effect would follow as in the case of the mine. The circulating medium would be lowered in value, and goods would experience a proportionate rise. The equilibrium between that and other nations would only be restored by the exportation of part of the coin.

The establishment of the bank, and the consequent issue of its notes, therefore, as well as the discovery of the mine, operate as an inducement to the exportation either of bullion, or of coin, and are beneficial only in as far as that object may be accomplished. The bank substitutes a currency of no value for one most costly, and enables us to turn the precious metals (which, though a very necessary part of our capital, yield no revenue), into a capital which will yield one. Dr. Smith compares the advantages attending the establishment of a bank to those which would be obtained by converting our highways into pastures and corn fields, and procuring a road through the air. The highways, like the coin, are highly useful, but neither yield any revenue. Some people might be alarmed at the specie leaving the country, and might consider that as a disadvantageous trade which required us to part with it; indeed the law so considers it by its enactments against the exportation of specie; but a very little reflection will convince us that it is our choice, and not our necessity, that sends it abroad; and that it is highly beneficial to us to exchange that commodity which is superfluous, for others which may be made productive.

The exportation of the specie may at all times be safely left to the discretion of individuals; it will not be exported more than any other commodity, unless its exportation should be advantageous to the country. If it be advantageous to export it, no laws can effectually prevent its exportation. Happily, in this case, as well as in most others in commerce, where there is free competition, the interests of the individual and that of the community are never at variance.

Were it possible to carry the law against melting, or exporting of coin, into strict execution, at the same time that the exportation of gold bullion was freely allowed, no advantage could accrue from it, but great injury must arise to those who might have to pay, possibly, two ounces or more of coined gold for one of uncoined gold. This would be a real depreciation of our currency, raising the prices of all other commodities in the same proportion as it increased that of gold bullion. The owner of money would in this case suffer an injury equal to what a proprietor of corn would suffer, were a law to be passed prohibiting him from selling his corn for more than half its market value. The law against the exportation of the coin has this tendency, but is so easily evaded, that gold in bullion has always been nearly of the same value as gold in coin.

Thus, then, it appears that the currency of one country can never for any length of time be much more valuable, as far as equal quantities of the precious metals are concerned, than that of another; that excess of currency is but a relative term; that is the circulation of England were ten millions, that of France five millions, that of Holland four millions, etc. whilst they kept their proportions, though the currency of each country were doubled or trebled, neither country would be conscious of an excess of currency. The prices of commodities would every where rise, on account of the increase of currency, but there would be no exportation of money from either. But if these proportions be destroyed by England alone doubling her currency, while that of France, Holland, etc. continued as before, we should then be conscious of an excess in our currency, and for the same reason the other countries would feel a deficiency in theirs, and part of our excess would be exported till the proportions, of ten, five, four, etc. were again established.

If in France an ounce of gold were more valuable than in England, and would therefore in France purchase more of any commodity common to both countries, gold would immediately quit England for such purpose, and we should send gold in preference to any thing else, because it would be the cheapest exchangeable commodity in the English market; for if gold be dearer in France than in England, goods must be cheaper; we should not therefore send them from the dear to the cheap market, but, on the contrary, they would come from the cheap to the dear market, and would be exchanged for our gold.

The Bank might continue to issue their notes, and the specie be exported with advantage to the country, while their notes were payable in specie on demand, because they could never issue more notes than the value of the coin which would have circulated had there been no bank.[1]

If they attempted to exceed this amount, the excess would be immediately returned to them for specie; because our currency, being thereby diminished in value, could be advantageously exported, and could not be retained in our circulation. These are the means, as I have already explained, by which our currency endeavors to equalize itself with the currencies of other countries. As soon as this equality was attained, all advantage arising from exportation would cease; but if the Bank, assuming that because a given quantity of circulating medium had been necessary last year, therefore the same quantity must be necessary this, or for any other reason, continued to re-issue the returned notes, the stimulus which a redundant currency first gave to the exportation of the coin would be again renewed with similar effects; gold would be again demanded, the exchange would become un-favourable, and gold bullion would rise, in a small degree, above its mint price, because it is legal to export bullion, but illegal to export the coin, and the difference would be about equal to the fair compensation for the risk.

In this manner, if the Bank persisted in returning their notes into circulation, every guinea might be drawn out of their coffers.

If, to supply the deficiency of their stock of gold, they were to purchase gold bullion at the advanced price, and have it coined into guineas, this would not remedy the evil; guineas would be still de-manded, but, instead of being exported, would be melted, and sold to the Bank as bullion at the advanced price. "The operations of the Bank," observed Dr. Smith, alluding to an analogous case, "were, upon this account, somewhat like the web of Penelope,—the work that was done in the day was undone in the night." The same sentiment is expressed by Mr. Thornton: "Finding the guineas in their coffers to lessen every day, they must naturally be supposed to be desirous of replacing them by all effectual and not extravagantly expensive means. They will be disposed, to a certain degree, to buy gold, though at a losing price, and to coin it into new guineas; but they will have to do this at the very moment when many are privately melting what is coined. The one party will be melting and selling while the other is buying and coining. And each of these two contending businesses will now be carried on, not on account of an actual exportation of each melted guinea to Hamburgh, but the operation, or at least a great part of it, will be confined to Lon-don, the coiners and the melters living on the same spot, and giving constant employment to each other.

"The Bank," continues Mr. Thornton, "if we suppose it, as we now do, to carry on this sort of contest with the melters, is obviously waging a very unequal war; and even though it should not be tired early, it will be likely to be tired sooner than its adversaries."

The Bank would be obliged, therefore, ultimately to adopt the only remedy in their power to put a stop to the demand for guineas. They would withdraw part of their notes from circulation, till they should have increased the value of the remainder to that of gold bullion, and, consequently, to the value of the currencies of other countries. All advantage from the exportation of gold bullion would then cease, and there would be no temptation to exchange bank notes for guineas.

In this view of the subject, then, it appears that the temptation to export money in exchange for goods, or what is termed an unfavourable balance of trade, never arises but from a redundant currency. But Mr. Thornton, who has considered this subject very much at large, supposes that a very unfavourable balance of trade may be occasioned to this country by a bad harvest, and the consequent importation of corn; and that there may be at the same time an unwillingness in the country to which we are indebted to receive our goods in payment; the balance due to the foreign country must therefore be paid out of that part of our currency consisting of coin, and that hence arises the demand for gold bullion, and its increased price. He considers the Bank as affording considerable accommodation to the merchants, by supplying with their notes the void occasioned by the exportation of the specie.

As it is acknowledged by Mr. Thornton, in many parts of his work, that the price of gold bullion is rated in gold coin, and as it is also acknowledged by him that the law against melting gold coin into bullion, and exporting it, is easily evaded, it follows, that no demand for gold bullion, arising from this or any other cause, can raise the money price of that commodity. The error of this reasoning proceeds from not distinguishing between an increase in the value of gold, and an increase in its money price.

If there were a great demand for corn, its money price would advance, because, in comparing corn with money, we in fact compare it with another commodity; and, for the same reason, when there is a great demand for gold, its corn price will increase; but in neither case will a bushel of corn be worth more than a bushel of corn, or an ounce of gold more than an ounce of gold. An ounce of gold bullion could not, whatever the demand might be, whilst its price was rated in gold coin, be of more value than an ounce of coined gold, or 3l. 17s. 10½d.

If this argument should not be considered as conclusive, I should urge that a void in the currency, as here supposed, can only be occasioned by the annihilation or limitation of paper currency, and then it would speedily be filled by importations of bullion, which its increased value, in consequence of the diminution of circulating medium, would infallibly attract to the advantageous market. However great the scarcity of corn might be, the exportation of money would be limited by its increasing scarcity. Money is in such general demand, and, in the present state of civilization, is so essential to commercial transactions, that it can never be exported to excess; even in a war, such as the present, when our enemy endeavors to interdict all commerce with us, the value which the currency would bear from its increasing scarcity would prevent the exportation of it from being carried so far as to occasion a void in the circulation.

Mr. Thornton has not explained to us why any unwillingness should exist in the foreign country to receive our goods in exchange for their corn; and it would be necessary for him to show, that if such an unwillingness were to exist, we should agree to indulge it so far as to consent to part with our coin.

If we consent to give coin in exchange for goods, it must be from choice, not necessity. We should not import more goods than we export, unless we had a redundancy of currency, which it therefore suits us to make a part of our exports. The exportation of the coin is caused by its cheapness, and is not the effect, but the cause of an unfavourable balance: We should not export it, if we did not send it to a better market, or if we had any commodity which we could export more profitably. It is a salutary remedy for a redundant currency; and as I have already endeavored to prove that redundancy or excess is only a relative term, it follows that the demand for it abroad arises only from the comparative deficiency of the currency of the importing country, which there causes its superior value.

It resolves itself entirely into a question of interest. If the sellers of the corn of England, to the amount, I will suppose, of a million, could import goods which cost a million in England, but would produce, when sold abroad, more than if the million had been sent in money, goods would be preferred; if otherwise, money would be demanded.

It is only after a comparison of the value in their markets and in our own of gold and other commodities, and because gold is cheaper in the London market than in theirs, that foreigners prefer gold in exchange for their corn. If we diminish the quantity of currency, we give an additional value to it: This will induce them to alter their election, and prefer the commodities. If I owed a debt in Hamburgh of 100l., I should endeavor to find out the cheapest mode of paying it. If I send money, the expense attending its transportation being, I will suppose, 5l., to discharge my debt will cost me 105l. If I purchase cloth here, which, with the expenses attending its exportation, will cost me 106l., and

69

which will in Hamburgh sell for 100l., it is evidently more to my advantage to send the money. If the purchase and expenses of sending hardware to pay my debt will take 107l., I should prefer sending cloth to hardware, but I would send neither in preference to money, because money would be the cheapest exportable commodity in the London market. The same reasons would operate with the exporter of the corn, if the transaction were on his own account. But if the Bank, "fearful for the safety of their establishment," and knowing that the requisite number of guineas would be withdrawn from their coffers at the mint price, should think it necessary to diminish the amount of their notes in circulation, the proportion between the value of the money, of the cloth, and of the hardware, would no longer be as 105, 106, and 107; but the money would become the most valuable of the three, and therefore would be less advantageously employed in discharging the foreign debts.

If, which is a much stronger case, we agreed to pay a subsidy to a foreign power, money would not be exported whilst there were any goods which could more cheaply discharge the payment. The interest of individuals would render the exportation of the money unnecessary.[2]

Thus, then, specie will be sent abroad to discharge a debt only when it is superabundant; only when it is the cheapest exportable commodity. If the Bank were at such a time paying their notes in specie, gold would be demanded for that purpose. It would be obtained there at its mint price, whereas its price as bullion would be something above its value as coin, because bullion could, and coin could not, be legally exported.

It is evident, then, that a depreciation of the circulating medium is the necessary consequence of its redundance; and that in the common state of the national currency this depreciation is counteracted by the exportation of the precious metals.[3]

Such, then, appear to me to be the laws that regulate the distribution of the precious metals throughout the world, and which cause and limit their circulation from one country to another, by regulating their value in each. But before I proceed to examine on these principles the main object of my inquiry, it is necessary that I should show what is the standard measure of value in this country, and of which, therefore, our paper currency ought to be the representative, because it can only be by a comparison to this standard that its regularity, or its depreciation, may be estimated.

No permanent[4] measure of value can be said to exist in any nation while the circulating medium consists of two metals, because they are constantly subject to vary in value with respect to each other. However exact the conductors of the mint may be, in proportioning the relative value of gold to silver in the coins, at the time when they fix the ratio, they cannot prevent one of these metals from rising, while the other remains stationary, or falls in value. Whenever this happens, one of the coins will be melted to be sold for the other. Mr. Locke, Lord Liverpool, and many other writers, have ably considered this subject, and have all agreed, that the only remedy for the evils in the currency proceeding from this source, is the making one of the metals only the standard measure of value. Mr. Locke considered silver as the most proper metal for this purpose, and proposed that gold coins should be left to find their own value, and pass for a greater or lesser number of shillings, as the market price of gold might vary with respect to silver.

Lord Liverpool, on the contrary, maintained that gold was not only the most proper metal for a general measure of value in this country, but that, by the common consent of the people, it had become so, was so considered by foreigners, and that it was best suited to the increased commerce and wealth of England.

He, therefore, proposed, that gold coin only should be a legal tender for sums exceeding one guinea, and silver coins for sums not exceeding that amount. As the law now stands, gold coin is a legal tender for all sums; but it was enacted in the year 1774, "That no tender in payment of money made in the silver coin of this realm, of any sum exceeding the sum of twenty-five pounds at any one time, shall be reputed in law, or allowed to be legal tender within Great Britain or Ireland, for more than according to its value by weight, after the rate of 5s. 2d. for each ounce of silver." The same regulation was revived in 1798, and is now in force.

For many reasons given by Lord Liverpool, it appears, proved beyond dispute, that gold coin has been for near a century the principal measure of value; but this is, I think, to be attributed to the inaccurate determination of the mint proportions. Gold has been valued too high; no silver, therefore, can remain in circulation which is of its standard weight.

If a new regulation were to take place, and silver to be valued too high, or (which is the same thing) if the market proportions between the prices of gold and silver were to become greater than those of the mint, gold would then disappear, and silver become the standard currency.

This may require further explanation. The relative value of gold and silver in the coins is as 15 9/124 to one. An ounce of gold which is coined into 3l. 17s. 10½d. of gold coin, is worth, according to the mint regulation, 15 9/124 ounces of silver, because that weight of silver is also coined into 3l. 17s. 10½d. of silver coin. Whilst the relative value of gold to silver is in the market under fifteen to one, which it has been for a great number of years till lately, gold coin would necessarily be the standard measure of value, because neither the Bank nor any individual would send 15 9/124 ounces of silver to the mint to be coined into 3l. 17s. 10½d., when they could sell that quantity of silver in the market for more than 3l. 17s. 10½d. in gold coin; and this they could do by the supposition, that less than fifteen ounces of silver would purchase an ounce of gold.

But if the relative value of gold to silver be more than the mint proportion of 15 9/124 to one, no gold would then be sent to the mint to be coined, because as either of the metals are a legal tender to any amount, the possessor of an ounce of gold would not send it to the mint to be coined into 3l. 17s. 10½d. of gold coin, whilst he could sell it, which he could do in such a case, for more than 3l. 17s. 10½d. of silver coin. Not only would not gold be carried to the mint to be coined, but the illicit trader would melt the gold coin, and sell it as bullion for more than its nominal value in the silver coin. Thus, then, gold would disappear from circulation, and silver coin become the standard measure of value. As gold has lately experienced a considerable rise compared with silver (an ounce of standard gold, which, on an average of many years, was of equal value to 14¾ ounces of standard silver, being now in the market of the same value as 15½ ounces), this would be the case now were the Bank Restriction-bill repealed, and the coinage of silver freely allowed at the mint, in the same manner as that of gold; but in an act of Parliament of 39 Geo. III is the following clause:

"Whereas inconvenience may arise from any coinage of silver until such regulations may be formed as shall appear necessary; and whereas from the present low price of silver bullion, owing to temporary circumstances, a small quantity of silver bullion has been brought to the mint to be coined, and there is reason to suppose that a still further quantity may be brought; and it is, therefore, necessary to suspend the coining of silver for the present; be it therefore enacted, That from and after the passing of this act, no silver bullion shall be coined at the mint, nor shall any silver coin that may have been coined there be delivered, any law to the contrary notwithstanding."

This law is now in force. It would appear, therefore, to have been the intention of the legislature to establish gold as the standard of currency in this country. Whilst this law is in force, silver coin must be confined to small payments only, the quantity in circulation being barely sufficient for that purpose. It might be for the interest of a debtor to pay his large debts in silver coin if he could get silver bullion coined into money; but being prevented by the above law from doing so, he is necessarily obliged to discharge his debt with gold coin, which he could obtain at the mint with gold bullion to any amount. Whilst this law is in force, gold must always continue to be the standard of currency.

Were the market value of an ounce of gold to become equal to thirty ounces of silver, gold would nevertheless be the measure of value, whilst this prohibition continued in force. It would be of no avail, that the possessor of thirty ounces of silver should know that he once could have discharged a debt of 3l. 17s. 10½d. by procuring 15 9/124 ounces of silver to be coined at the mint, as he would in this case have no other means of discharging his debt but by selling his thirty ounces of silver at the market value, that is to say, for one ounce of gold, or 3l. 17s. 10½d. of gold coin.

The public has sustained, at different times, very serious loss from the depreciation of the circulating medium, arising from the unlawful practice of clipping the coins.

In proportion as they become debased, so the prices of every commodity for which they are exchangeable rise in nominal value, not excepting gold and silver bullion: accordingly we find, that before the re-coinage in the reign of King William the Third, the silver currency had become so degraded, that an ounce of silver, which ought to be contained in sixty-two pence, sold for seventy-seven pence; and a guinea, which was valued at the mint at twenty shillings, passed in all contracts for thirty shillings. This evil was then remedied by the re-coinage. Similar effects followed from the debasement of the gold currency, which were again corrected in 1774 by the same means.

Our gold coins have, since 1774, continued nearly at their standard purity; but our silver currency has again become debased. By an assay at the mint in 1798, it appears that our shillings were found to be twenty-four per cent, and our sixpences thirty-eight per cent, under their mint value; and I am informed, that by a late experiment they were found considerably more deficient. They do not, therefore, contain as much pure silver as they did in the reign of King William. This debasement, however, did not operate previously to 1798, as on the former occasion.

At that time both gold and silver bullion rose in proportion to the debasement of the silver coin. All foreign exchanges were against us full twenty per cent., and many of them still more. But although the debasement of the silver coin had continued for many years, it had neither, previously to 1798, raised the price of gold nor silver, nor had it produced any effect on the exchanges. This is a convincing proof, that gold coin was, during that period, considered as the standard measure of value. Any debasement of the gold coin would then have produced the same effects on the prices of gold and silver bullion, and on the foreign exchanges, which were formerly caused by the debasement of the silver coins.[5]

While the currency of different countries consists of the precious metals, or of a paper money which is at all times exchangeable for them; and while the metallic currency is not debased by wearing or clipping, a comparison of the weight and degree of fineness of their coins will enable us to ascertain their par of exchange. Thus the par of exchange between Holland and England is stated to be about eleven florins, because the pure silver contained in eleven florins is equal to the pure silver contained in twenty standard shillings.

This par is not, nor can it be, absolutely fixed; because gold coin being the standard of commerce in England, and silver coin in Holland, a pound sterling, or 20/21 of a guinea, may at different times be more or less valuable than twenty standard shillings, and therefore more or less valuable than its equivalent of eleven florins. Estimating the par either by silver or by gold will be sufficiently exact for our purpose.

If I owe a debt in Holland, by knowing the par of exchange, I also know the quantity of our money which will be necessary to discharge it.

If my debt amount to eleven hundred florins, and gold have not varied in value, 100l. in our pure gold coin will purchase as much Dutch currency as is necessary to pay my debt. By exporting the 100l. therefore in coin, or (which is the same thing) paying a bullion merchant the 100l. in coin, and allowing him the expenses attending its transportation, such as freight, insurance, and his profit, he will sell me a bill which will discharge my debt; at the same time he will export the bullion to enable his correspondent to pay the bill when it shall become due.

These expenses, then, are the utmost limits of an unfavourable exchange. However great my debt may be, though it equaled the largest subsidy ever given by this country to an ally; while I could pay the bullion merchant in coin of standard value, he would be glad to export it, and to sell me bills. But if I pay him for his bill in a debased coin, or in a depreciated paper money, he will not be willing to sell me his bill at this rate; because if the coin be debased it does not contain the quantity of pure gold or silver which ought to be contained in 100l., and he must therefore export an additional number of such debased pieces of money to enable him to pay my debt of 100l., or its equivalent, eleven hundred florins. If I pay him in paper money, as he cannot send it a-broad, he will consider whether it will purchase as much gold or silver bullion as is contained in the coin for which it is a substitute; if it will do this, paper will be as acceptable to him as coin; but if it will not, he will expect a further premium for his bill, equal to the depreciation of the paper.

While the circulating medium consists, therefore, of coin unde-based, or of paper money immediately exchangeable for undebased coin, the exchange can never be more above, or more below par, than the expenses attending the transportation of the precious metals. But when it consists of a depreciated paper money, it necessarily will fall according to the degree of the depreciation.

The exchange will, therefore, be a tolerably accurate criterion by which we may judge of the debasement of the currency, proceeding either from a clipped coinage or a depreciated paper money.

It is observed by Sir James Stuart, "That if the foot measure was altered at once over all England, by adding to it or taking from it any proportional part of its standard length, the alteration would be best discovered by comparing the new foot with that of Paris, or of any other country which had suffered no alteration.

"Just so, if the pound sterling, which is the English unit, shall be found any how changed, and if the variation it has met with be difficult to ascertain because of a complication of circumstances, the best way to discover it will be to compare the former and the present value of it with the money of other nations which has suffered no variation. This the exchange will perform with the greatest exactness."

The Edinburgh reviewers, in speaking of Lord King's pamphlet, observe, that "it does not follow because our imports always consist partly of bullion that the balance of trade is therefore permanently in our favour. Bullion," they say, "is a commodity for which, as for every other, there is a varying demand, and which, exactly like any other, may enter the catalogue either of imports or exports; and this exportation or importation of bullion will not affect the course of exchange in a different way from the exportation or importation of any other commodities."

No person ever exports or imports bullion without first considering the rate of exchange. It is by the rate of exchange that he discovers the relative value of bullion in the two countries between which it is estimated. It is therefore consulted by the bullion merchant in the same manner as the price-current is by other merchants, before they determine on the exportation or importation of other commodities. If eleven florins in Holland contain an equal quantity of pure silver as twenty standard shillings, silver bullion, equal in weight to twenty standard shillings, can never be exported from London to Amsterdam whilst the exchange is at par, or unfavourable to Holland. Some expense and risk must attend its exportation, and the very term *par* expresses that a quantity of silver bullion, equal to that weight and purity, is to be obtained in Holland by the purchase of a bill of exchange, free of all expense. Who would send bullion to Holland at an expense of three or four per cent when, by the purchase of a bill at par, he in fact obtains an order for the delivery to his correspondent in Holland of the same weight of bullion which he was about to export?

It would be as reasonable to contend that, when the price of corn is higher in England than on the continent, corn would be sent, notwithstanding all the charges on its exportation, to be sold in the cheaper market.

Having already noticed the disorders to which a metallic currency is exposed, I will proceed to consider those which, though not caused by the debased state of either the gold or silver coins, are nevertheless more serious in their ultimate consequences.

Our circulating medium is almost wholly composed of paper, and it behooves us to guard against the depreciation of the paper currency with at least as much vigilance as against that of the coins.

This we have neglected to do.

Parliament, by restricting the Bank from paying in specie, have enabled the conductors of that concern to increase or decrease at pleasure the quantity and amount of their notes; and the previously existing checks against an over-issue having been thereby removed, those conductors have acquired the power of increasing or decreasing the value of the paper currency.

In tracing the present evils to their source, and proving their existence by an appeal to the two unerring tests I have before mentioned, namely, the rate of exchange and the price of bullion, I shall avail myself of the account given by Mr. Thornton of the conduct of the Bank before the restriction, to show how clearly they acted on the principle which he has expressly acknowledged, viz. that the value of their notes is dependent on their amount, and that they ascertained the variation in their value by the tests I have just referred to.

Mr. Thornton tells us, "That if at any time the exchanges of the country become so unfavourable as to produce a material excess of the market above the mint price of gold, the directors of the Bank, as appears by the evidence of some of their body given to Parliament, were disposed to resort to a reduction of their paper, as a means of diminishing or removing the excess, and of thus providing for the security of their establishment. They, moreover, have at all times," he says, "been accustomed to observe some limit as to the quantity of their notes for the same prudential reasons." And in another place: "When the price which our coin will fetch in foreign countries is such as to tempt it out of the kingdom, the directors of the Bank naturally diminish, in some degree, the quantity of their paper through an anxiety for the safety of their establishment. By diminishing their paper, they raise its value; and in raising its value, they raise also the value in England of the current coin which is exchanged for it. Thus, the value of our gold coin conforms itself to the value of the current paper, and the current paper is rendered by the Bank directors of that value which it is necessary that it should bear in order to prevent large exportations; a value sometimes rising a little above, and sometimes falling a little below, the price which our coin bears abroad."

The necessity which the Bank felt itself under to guard the safety of its establishment, therefore, always prevented, before the restriction from paying in specie, a too lavish issue of paper money.

Thus we find that, for a period of twenty-three years previously to the suspension of cash payments in 1797, the average price of gold bullion was 3l. 17s. 7¾d. per ounce, about 2¾d. under the Mint price; and for sixteen years previously to 1774, it never was much above 4l. per ounce. It should be remembered, that during these sixteen years our gold coin was debased by wearing, and it is therefore probable that 4l. of such debased money did not weigh as much as the ounce of gold for which it was exchanged.

Dr. Smith considers every permanent excess of the market above the mint price of gold, as referable to the state of the coins. While the coin was of its standard weight and purity, the market price of gold bullion, he thought, could not greatly exceed the Mint price.

Mr. Thornton contends that this cannot be the only cause. "We have," he says, "lately experienced fluctuations in our exchanges, and correspondent variations in the market, compared with the mint price of gold, amounting to no less than eight or ten per cent; the state of our coinage continuing in all respects the same." Mr. Thornton should have reflected, that at the time he wrote, specie could not be demanded at the Bank in exchange for notes; that this was a cause for the depreciation of the currency which Dr. Smith could never have anticipated. If Mr. Thornton had proved that there had been a fluctuation of ten per cent in the price of gold, while the Bank paid their notes in specie, and the coin was undebased, he would then have convicted Dr. Smith of "having treated this important subject in a defective and unsatisfactory manner."[6]

But as all checks against the over-issues of the Bank are now removed by the act of Parliament, which restricts them from paying their notes in specie, they are no longer bound by "fears for the safety of their establishment," to limit the quantity of their notes to that sum which shall keep them of the same value as the coin which they represent. Accordingly, we find that gold bullion has risen from 3l. 17s. 7¾d., the average price previously to 1797, to 4l. 10s., and has been lately as high as 4l. 13. per ounce.

We may, therefore, fairly conclude, that this difference in the relative value, or, in other words, that this depreciation in the actual value of bank notes has been caused by the too abundant quantity which the Bank has sent into circulation. The same cause which has produced a difference of from fifteen to twenty per cent in bank notes when compared with gold bullion, may increase it to fifty per cent. There can be no limit to the depreciation which may arise from a constantly increasing quantity of paper. The stimulus which a redundant currency gives to the exportation of the coin has acquired new force, but cannot, as formerly, which is necessarily confined to ourselves. Every increase in its quantity degrades it below the value of gold and silver bullion, below the value of the currencies of other countries.

The effect is the same as that which would have been produced from clipping our coins.

If one fifth were taken off from every guinea, the market price of gold bullion would rise one fifth above the mint price. Forty-four guineas and a half (the number of guineas weighing a pound, and therefore called the mint price), would no longer weigh a pound, therefore a fifth more than that quantity, or about 56l. would be the price of a pound of gold, and the difference between the market and the mint price, between 56l. and 46l. 14s. 6d. would measure the depreciation.

If such debased coin were to continue to be called by the name of guineas, and if the value of gold bullion and all other commodities were rated in the debased coin, a guinea fresh from the mint would be said to be worth 1l. 5s., and that sum would be given for it by the illicit trader; but it would not be the value of the new guinea which had increased, but that of the debased guineas which had fallen. This would immediately be evident, if a proclamation were issued, prohibiting the debased guineas from being current but by weight at the mint price of 3l. 17s. 10½d.; this would be constituting the new and heavy guineas the standard measure of value, in lieu of the clipped and debased guineas. The latter would then pass at their true value, and be called seventeen or eighteen shilling pieces. So if a proclamation to the same effect were now enforced, bank notes would not be less current, but would pass only for the value of the gold bullion which they would purchase. A guinea would then no longer be said to be worth 1l. 5s., but a pound note would be current only for sixteen or seventeen shillings. At present gold coin is only a commodity, and bank notes are the standard measure of value, but in that case gold coin would be that measure, and bank notes would be the marketable commodity.

"It is," says Mr. Thornton, "the maintenance of our general exchanges, or, in other words, it is the agreement of the mint price with the bullion price of gold, which seems to be the true proof that the circulating paper is not depreciated."

When the motive for exporting gold occurs, while the Bank does not pay in specie, and gold cannot therefore be obtained at its mint price, the small quantity that can be procured will be collected for exportation, and bank notes will be sold at a discount for gold in proportion to their excess. In saying, however, that gold is at a high price, we are mistaken; it is not gold, it is paper which has changed its value. Compare an ounce of gold, or 3l. 17s. 10½d. to commodities, it bears the same proportion to them which it has before done; and if it does not, it is preferable to increased taxation, or to some of those causes which are so constantly operating on its value. But if we compare the substitute of an ounce of gold, 3l. 17s. 10½d. in bank notes, with commodities, we shall then discover the depreciation of the bank notes. In every market of the world I am obliged to part with 4l. 10s. in bank notes to purchase the same quantity of commodities which I can obtain for the gold that is in 3l. 17s. 10½d. of coin.

It is often asserted, that a guinea is worth at Hamburgh twenty-six or twenty-eight shillings; but we should be very much deceived if we should therefore conclude that a guinea could be sold at Hamburgh for as much silver as is contained in twenty-six or twenty-eight shillings. Before the alteration in the relative value of gold and silver, a guinea would not sell at Hamburgh for as much silver coin as is contained in twenty-one standard shillings; it will at the present market price sell for a sum of silver currency, which, if imported and carried to our mint to be coined, will produce in our standard silver coin 21s. 5d.[7]

It is nevertheless true, that the same quantity of silver will, at Hamburgh, purchase a bill payable in London, in bank notes, for twenty-six or twenty-eight shillings. Can there be a more satisfactory proof of the depreciation of our circulating medium?

It is said, that, if the Restriction-bill were not in force, every guinea would leave the country.[8]

This is, no doubt, true; but if the Bank were to diminish the quantity of their notes until they had increased their value fifteen per cent, the restriction might be safely removed, as there would then be no temptation to export specie. However long it may be deferred, however great may be the discount on their notes, the Bank can never resume their payments in specie, until they first reduce the amount of their notes in circulation to these limits.

The law is allowed by all writers on political economy to be a useless barrier against the exportation of guineas: It is so easily evaded, that it is doubted whether it has had the effect of keeping a single guinea more in England than there would have been without such law. Mr. Locke, Sir J. Stuart, Dr. Smith, Lord Liverpool, and Mr. Thornton, all agree on this subject. The latter gentleman observes, "that the state of the British law unquestionably serves to discourage and limit, though not effectually to hinder, that exportation of guineas which is encouraged by an unfavourable balance of trade, and perhaps scarcely lessens it when the profit on exportation becomes very great." Yet, after every guinea that can in the present state of things be procured by the illicit trader has been melted and exported, he will hesitate before he openly buys guineas with bank notes at a premium, because, though considerable profit may attend such speculation, he will thereby render himself an object of suspicion. He may be watched, and prevented from effecting his object. As the penalties of the law are severe, and the temptation to informers great, secrecy is essential to his operations. When guineas can be procured by merely sending a bank note for them to the Bank, the law will be easily evaded; but when it is necessary to collect them openly and from a widely diffused circulation, consisting almost wholly of paper, the advantage attending it must be very considerable before any one will encounter the risk of being detected.

When we reflect that above sixty millions sterling have been coined into guineas during his present Majesty's reign, we may form some idea of the extent to which the exportation of gold must have been carried. But repeal the law against the exportation of guineas, permit them to be openly sent out of the country, and what can prevent an ounce of standard gold in guineas from selling at as good a price for bank notes as an ounce of Portuguese gold coin, or standard gold in bars, when it is known to be equal to them in fineness? And if an ounce of standard gold in guineas would sell in the market, as standard bars do now, at 4l. 10s. per ounce, or, as they have lately done, at 4l. 13s. per ounce, what shopkeeper would sell his goods at the same price either for gold or bank notes indifferently? If the price of a coat were 3l. 17s. 10½d. or an ounce of gold, and if at the same time an ounce of gold would sell for 4l. 13s., is it conceivable that it would be a matter of indifference to the tailor whether he were paid in gold or in bank notes?

It is only because a guinea will not purchase more than a pound note and a shilling that many hesitate to allow that bank notes are at a discount. The *Edinburgh Review* supports the same opinion; but, if my reasoning be correct, I have shown such objections to be groundless.

Mr. Thornton has told us that an unfavourable trade will account for an unfavourable exchange; but we have already seen that in unfavourable trade, if such be an accurate term, is limited in its effects on the exchange. That limit is probably four or five per cent. This will not account for a depreciation of fifteen or twenty per cent. Moreover, Mr. Thornton has told us, and I entirely agree with him, "that it may be laid down as a general truth, that the commercial exports and imports of a state naturally proportion themselves in some degree to each other, and that the balance of trade, therefore, cannot continue for a very long time to be either highly favourable or highly unfavourable to a country." Now, the low exchange, so far from being temporary, existed before Mr. Thornton wrote in 1802, and has since been progressively increasing, and is now from fifteen to twenty per cent against us. Mr. Thornton must therefore, according to his own principles, attribute it to some more permanent cause than an unfavourable balance of trade, and will, I doubt not, whatever his opinion may formerly have been, now agree that it is to be accounted for only by the depreciation of the circulating medium.

It can, I think, no longer be disputed that bank notes are at a discount. While the price of gold bullion is 4l. 10s. per ounce, or, in other words, while any man will consent to give that which professes to be an obligation to pay nearly an ounce and a sixth of an ounce of gold for an ounce, it cannot be contended that 4l. 10s. in notes and 4l. 10s. in gold coin are of the same value.

An ounce of gold is coined into 3l. 17s. 10½d.; by possessing that sum, therefore, I have an ounce of gold, and would not give 4l. 10s. in gold coin, or notes which I could immediately exchange for 4l. 10s., for an ounce of gold.

It is contrary to common sense to suppose that such could be the market value, unless the price were estimated in a depreciated medium.

If the price of gold were estimated in silver, indeed, the price might rise to 4l., 5l., or 10l. an ounce, and it would of itself be no proof of the depreciation of paper currency, but of an alteration in the relative value of gold and silver. I have, however, I think, proved that silver is not the standard measure of value, and therefore not the medium in which the value of gold is estimated. But if it were, as an ounce of gold is only worth in the market fifteen and one half ounces of silver, and as fifteen and one half ounces of silver is precisely equal in weight, and is therefore coined into eighty shillings, an ounce of gold ought not to sell for more than 4l.

Those, then, who maintain that silver is the measure of value, cannot prove that any demand for gold which may have taken place, from whatever cause it may have proceeded, can have raised its price above 4l. per ounce. All above that price must, on their own principles, be called a depreciation in the value of bank notes. It therefore follows, that if bank notes be the representative of silver coin, then an ounce of gold, selling as it now does for 4l. 10s., sells for an amount of notes which represent seventeen ounces and a half of silver, whereas, in the bullion market, it can only be exchanged for fifteen ounces and a half. Fifteen ounces and a half of silver bullion are therefore of equal value with an engagement of the Bank to pay to bearer seventeen ounces and a half.

The market price of silver is at the present time 5s. 9½d. per ounce, estimated in bank notes, the mint price being only 5s. 2d., consequently, the standard silver in 100l. is worth more than 112l. in bank notes.

But bank notes, it may be said, are the representatives of our debased silver coin, and not of our standard silver. This is not true, because the law which I have already quoted declares silver to be a legal tender for sums only not exceeding 25l., except by weight. If the Bank insisted on paying the holder of a bank note of 1000l. in silver coin, they would be bound either to give him standard silver of full weight, or debased silver of an equal value, with the exception of 25l., which they might pay him in debased coin. But the 1000l., so consisting of 975l. pure money, and 25l. debased, is worth more than 1,112l. at the present market value of silver bullion.

It is said that the amount of bank notes has not increased in a greater proportion than the augmentation of our trade required, and therefore cannot be excessive. This assertion would be difficult to prove, and if true, no argument but what is delusive could be founded on it. In the first place, the daily improvements which we are making in the art of economizing the use of circulating medium by improved methods of banking, would render the same amount of notes excessive now which were necessary for the same state of commerce at a former period. Secondly, there is a constant competition between the Bank of England and the country banks to establish their notes, to the exclusion of those of their rivals, in every district where the country banks are established.

As the latter have more than doubled in number within very few years, is it not probable that their activity may have been crowned with success, in displacing with their own notes many of those of the Bank of England?

If this have happened, the same amount of Bank of England notes would now be excessive, which, with a less extended commerce, was before barely sufficient to keep our currency on a level with that of other countries. No just conclusion can, therefore, be drawn from the actual amount of bank notes in circulation, though the fact, if examined, would, I have no doubt, be found to be that the increase in the amount of bank notes, and the high price of gold, have usually accompanied each other.

It is doubted, whether two or three millions of bank notes (the sum which the Bank is supposed to have added to the circulation, over and above the amount which it will easily bear) could have had such effects as are ascribed to them; but it should be recollected, that the Bank regulate the amount of the circulation of all the country banks, and it is probable that, if the Bank increase their issues three millions, they enable the country banks to add more than three millions to the general circulation of England.

The money of a particular country is divided amongst its different provinces by the same rules as the money of the world is divided amongst the different nations of which it is composed. Each district will retain in its circulation such a proportionate share of the currency of the country as its trade, and consequently its payments, may require, compared to the trade of the whole; and no increase can take place in the circulating medium of one district, without being generally diffused, or calling forth a proportionable quantity in every other district. It is this which keeps a country bank note always of the same value as a Bank of England note. If in London, where Bank of England notes only are current, one million be added to the amount in circulation, the currency will become cheaper there than elsewhere, or goods will become dearer. Goods will, therefore, be sent from the country to the London market to be sold at the high prices, or, which is much more probable, the country banks will take advantage of the relative deficiency in the country currency, and increase the amount of their notes in the same proportion as the Bank of England had done; prices would then be generally, and not partially, affected.

In the same manner, if Bank of England notes be diminished one million, the comparative value of the currency of London will be increased, and the prices of goods diminished. A Bank of England note will then be more valuable than a country bank note, because it will be wanted to purchase goods in the cheap market; and as the country banks are obliged to give Bank of England notes for their own when demanded, they would be called upon for them till the quantity of country paper should be reduced to the same proportion which it before bore to the London paper, producing a corresponding fall in the prices of all goods for which it was exchangeable.

The country banks could never increase the amount of their notes, unless to fill up a relative deficiency in the country currency, caused by the increased issues of the Bank of England.[9] If they attempted it, the same check which compelled the Bank of England to withdraw part of their notes from circulation when they used to pay them on demand in specie, would oblige the country banks to adopt the same course. Their notes would, on account of the increased quantity, be rendered of less value than the Bank of England notes, in the same manner as Bank of England notes were rendered of less value than the guineas which they represented. They would therefore be exchanged for Bank of England notes until they were of the same value.

The Bank of England is the great regulator of the country paper. When they increase or decrease the amount of their notes, the country banks do the same; and in no case can country banks add to the general circulation unless the Bank of England shall have previously increased the amount of their notes.

It is contended, that the rate of interest, and not the price of gold or silver bullion, is the criterion by which we may always judge of the abundance of paper money; that if it were too abundant, interest would fall, and if not sufficiently so, interest would rise. It can, I think, be made manifest, that the rate of interest is not regulated by the abundance or scarcity of money, but by the abundance or scarcity of that part of capital not consisting of money.

"Money," observes Dr. Smith, "the great wheel of circulation, the great instrument of commerce, like all other instruments of trade, though it makes a part, and a very valuable part of the capital, makes no part of the revenue of the society to which it belongs; and though the metal pieces of which it is composed, in the course of their annual circulation, distribute to every man the revenue which properly belongs to him, they make themselves no part of that revenue.

"When we compute the quantity of industry which the circulating capital of any society can employ, we must always have regard to those parts of it only which consist in provisions, materials, and finished work: The other, which consists in money, and which serves only to circulate those three, must always be deducted. In order to put industry into motion, three things are requisite: materials to work upon, tools to work with, and the wages or recompense for the sake of which the work is done. Money is neither a material to work upon nor a tool to work with; and though the wages of the workman are commonly paid to him in money, his real revenue, like that of all other men, consists not in money, but in money's worth; not in the metal pieces, but what can be got for them."

And in other parts of his work, it is maintained, that the discovery of the mines in America, which so greatly increased the quantity of money, did not lessen the interest for the use of it; the rate of interest being regulated by the profits on the employment of capital, and not by the number or quality of the pieces of metal which are used to circulate its produce.

Mr. Hume has supported the same opinion. The value of the circulating medium of every country bears some proportion to the value of the commodities which it circulates. In some countries this proportion is much greater than in others and varies, on some occasions, in the same country. It depends upon the rapidity of circulation, upon the degree of confidence and credit existing between traders, and, above all, on the judicious operations of banking. In England, so many means of economizing the use of circulating medium have been adopted, that its value, compared with the value of the commodities which it circulates, is probably (during a period of confidence[10]) reduced to as small a proportion as is practicable. What that proportion may be has been variously estimated.

No increase or decrease of its quantity, whether consisting of gold, silver, or paper money, can increase or decrease its value above or below this proportion. If the mines cease to supply the annual consumption of the precious metals, money will become more valuable, and a smaller quantity will be employed as a circulating medium. The diminution in the quantity will be proportioned to the increase of its value. In like manner, if new mines be discovered, the value of the precious metals will be reduced, and an increased quantity used in the circulation; so that in either case the relative value of money to the commodities which it circulates will continue as before.

If, whilst the Bank paid their notes on demand in specie, they were to increase their quantity, they would produce little permanent effect on the value of the currency, because nearly an equal quantity of the coin would be withdrawn from circulation and exported.

If the Bank were restricted from paying their notes in specie, and all the coin had been exported, any excess of their notes would depreciate the value of the circulating medium in proportion to the excess. If twenty millions had been the circulation of England before the restriction, and four millions were added to it, the twenty-four millions would be of no more value than the twenty were before, provided commodities had remained the same, and there had been no corresponding exportation of coins; and if the Bank were successively to increase it to fifty or one hundred millions, the increased quantity would be all absorbed in the circulation of England, but would be, in all cases, depreciated to the value of the twenty millions.

I do not dispute, that if the Bank were to bring a large additional sum of notes into the market, and offer them on loan, but that they would for a time affect the rate of interest. The same effects would follow from the discovery of a hidden treasure of gold or silver coin. If the amount were large, the Bank, or the owner of the treasure, might not be able to lend the notes or the money at four, nor perhaps above three per cent; but having done so, neither the notes, nor the money, would be retained unemployed by the borrowers; they would be sent into every market, and would everywhere raise the prices of commodities, till they were absorbed in the general circulation. It is only during the interval of the issues of the Bank, and their effect on prices, that we should be sensible of an abundance of money; interest would, during that interval, be under its natural level; but as soon as the additional sum of notes or of money became absorbed in the general circulation, the rate of interest would be as high, and new loans would be demanded with as much eagerness as before the additional issues.

The circulation can never be over full. If it be one of gold and silver, any increase in its quantity will be spread over the world. If it be one of paper, it will diffuse itself only in the country where it is issued. Its effects on prices will then be only local and nominal, as a compensation by means of the exchange will be made to foreign purchasers.

To suppose that any increased issues of the Bank can have the effect of permanently lowering the rate of interest, and satisfying the demands of all borrowers, so that there will be none to apply for new loans, or that a productive gold or silver mine can have such an effect, is to attribute a power to the circulating medium which it can never possess. Banks would, if this were possible, become powerful engines indeed. By creating paper money, and lending it at three or two per cent under the present market rate of interest, the Bank would reduce the profits on trade in the same proportion; and if they were sufficiently patriotic to lend their notes at an interest no higher than necessary to pay the expenses of their establishment, profits would be still further reduced; no nation, but by similar means, could enter into competition with us, we should engross the trade of the world. To what absurdities would not such a theory lead us! Profits can only be lowered by a competition of capitals not consisting of circulating medium. As the increase of bank notes does not add to this species of capital, as it neither increases our exportable commodities, our machinery, or our raw materials, it cannot add to our profits nor lower interest.[11]

When any one borrows money for the purpose of entering into trade, he borrows it as a medium by which he can possess himself of "materials, provisions, etc.," to carry on that trade; and it can be of little consequence to him, provided he obtain the quantity of materials, etc., necessary, whether he be obliged to borrow a thousand, or ten thousand pieces of money. If he borrow ten thousand, the produce of his manufacture will be ten times the nominal value of what it would have been, had one thousand been sufficient for the same purpose. The capital actually employed in the country is necessarily limited to the amount of the "materials, provision, etc.," and might be made equally productive, though not with equal facility, if trade were carried on wholly by barter. The successive possessors of the circulating medium have the command over this capital: But however abundant may be the quantity of money or of bank notes; though it may increase the nominal prices of commodities; though it may distribute the productive capital in different proportions; though the Bank, by increasing the quantity of their notes, may enable A to carry on part of the business formerly engrossed by B and C, nothing will be added to the real revenue and wealth of the country. B and C may be injured, and A and the Bank may be gainers, but they will gain exactly what B and C lose. There will be a violent and an unjust transfer of property, but no benefit whatever will be gained by the community.

For these reasons I am of opinion that the funds are not indebted for their high price to the depreciation of our currency. Their price must be regulated by the general rate of interest given for money. If before the depreciation I gave thirty years' purchase for land, and twenty-five for an annuity in the stocks, I can, after the depreciation, give a larger sum for the purchase of land, without giving more years' purchase, because the produce of the land will sell for a greater nominal value in consequence of the depreciation; but as the annuity in the funds is paid in the depreciated medium, there can be no reason why I should give a greater nominal value for it after than before the depreciation.

If guineas were degraded by clipping to half their present value, every commodity as well as land would rise to double its present nominal value; but as the interest of the stocks would be paid in the degraded guineas, they would, on that account, experience no rise.

The remedy which I propose for all the evils in our currency, is that the Bank should gradually decrease the amount of their notes in circulation until they shall have rendered the remainder of equal value with the coins which they represent, or, in other words, till the prices of gold and silver bullion shall be brought down to their mint price. I am well aware that the total failure of paper credit would be attended with the most disastrous consequences to the trade and commerce of the country, and even its sudden limitation would occasion so much ruin and distress, that it would be highly inexpedient to have recourse to it as the means of restoring our currency to its just and equitable value.

If the Bank were possessed of more guineas than they had notes in circulation, they could not, without great injury to the country, pay their notes in specie, while the price of gold bullion continued greatly above the mint price, and the foreign exchanges unfavourable to us. The excess of our currency would be exchanged for guineas at the Bank, and exported, and would be suddenly withdrawn from circulation. Before, therefore, they can safely pay in specie, the excess of notes must be gradually withdrawn from circulation. If gradually done, little inconvenience would be felt; so that the principle were fairly admitted, it would be for future consideration whether the object should be accomplished in one year or in five. I am fully persuaded that we shall never restore our currency to its equitable state, but by this preliminary step, or by the total overthrow of our paper credit.

If the Bank directors had kept the amount of their notes within reasonable bounds; if they had acted up to the principle which they have avowed to have been that which regulated their issues when they were obliged to pay their notes in specie, namely, to limit their notes to that amount which should prevent the excess of the market above the mint price of gold, we should not have been now exposed to all the evils of a depreciated, and perpetually varying currency.

Though the Bank derive considerable advantage from the present system, though the price of their capital stock has nearly doubled since 1797, and their dividends have proportionally increased, I am ready to admit with Mr. Thornton, that the directors, as monied men, sustain losses in common with others by a depreciation of the currency, much more serious to them than any advantages which they may reap from it as proprietors of Bank stock. I do, therefore, acquit them of being influenced by interested motives, but their mistakes, if they are such, are in their effects quite as pernicious to the community.

The extraordinary powers with which they are entrusted enable them to regulate at their pleasure the price at which those who are possessed of a particular kind of property, called money, shall dispose of it. The Bank directors have imposed upon these holders of money all the evils of a maximum. Today it is their pleasure that 4l. 10s. shall pass for 3l. 17s. 10½d., tomorrow they may degrade 4l. 15s. to the same value, and in another year 10l. may not be worth more. By what an insecure tenure is property consisting of money or annuities paid in money held! What security has the public creditor that the interest on the public debt, which is now paid in a medium depreciated fifteen per cent, may not hereafter be paid in one degraded fifty per cent? The injury to private creditors is not less serious. A debt contracted in 1797 may now be paid with eighty-five per cent of its amount; and who shall say that the depreciation will go no further?

The following observations of Dr. Smith on this subject are so important, that I cannot but recommend them to the serious attention of all thinking men.

"The raising the denomination of the coin has been the most usual expedient by which a real public bankruptcy has been disguised under the appearance of a pretended payment. If a sixpence, for example, should, either by act of Parliament, or royal proclamation, be raised to the denomination of a shilling, and twenty sixpences to that of a pound sterling, the person who under the old denomination had borrowed twenty shillings, or near four ounces of silver, would, under the new, pay with twenty sixpences, or with something less than two ounces. A national debt of about a hundred and twenty millions, nearly the capital of the funded debt of Great Britain, might in this manner be paid with about sixty-four millions of our present money. It would indeed be a pretended payment only, and the creditors of the public would be defrauded of ten shillings in the pound of what was due to them. The calamity, too, would extend much further than to the creditors of the public, and those of every private person would suffer a proportionable loss; and this without any advantage, but in most cases with a great additional loss to the creditors of the public. If the creditors of the public, indeed, were generally much in debt to other people, they might in some measure compensate their loss by paying their creditors in the same coin in which the public had paid them. But in most countries the creditors of the public are the greater part of them wealthy people, who stand more in the relation of creditors than in that of debtors towards the rest of their fellow citizens. A pretended payment of this kind, therefore, instead of alleviating, aggravates in most cases the loss of the creditors of the public; and without any advantage to the public, extends the calamity to a great number of other innocent people. It occasions a general and most pernicious subversion of the fortunes of private people; enriching in most cases the idle and profuse debtor at the expense of the industrious and frugal creditor, and transporting a great part of the national capital from the hands which are likely to increase and improve it, to those which are likely to dissipate and destroy it. When it becomes necessary for a state to declare itself bankrupt, in the same manner as when it becomes necessary for an individual to do so, a fair, open, and avowed bankruptcy is always the measure which is both least dishonourable to the debtor, and least hurtful to the creditor. The honour of a state is surely very poorly provided for, when, in order to cover the disgrace of a real bankruptcy, it has recourse to a juggling trick of this kind, so easily seen through, and at the same time so extremely pernicious."

These observations of Dr. Smith on a debased money are equally applicable to a depreciated paper currency. He has enumerated but a few of the disastrous consequences which attend the debasement of the circulating medium, but he has sufficiently warned us against trying such dangerous experiments. It will be a circumstance ever to be lamented, if this great country, having before its eyes the consequences of a forced paper circulation in America and France, should persevere in a system pregnant with so much disaster. Let us hope that she will be more wise. It is said, indeed, that the cases are dissimilar; that the Bank of England is independent of government. If this were true, the evils of a superabundant circulation would not be less felt; but it may be questioned whether a bank lending many millions more to government than its capital and savings, can be called independent of that government.

When the order of council for suspending the cash payments became necessary in 1797, the run upon the Bank was, in my opinion, caused by political alarm alone, and not by a superabundant, or a deficient quantity (as some have supposed) of their notes in circulation.[12]

This is a danger to which the Bank, from the nature of its institution, is at all times liable. No prudence on the part of the directors could perhaps have averted it: But if their loans to government had been more limited; if the same amount of notes had been issued to the public through the medium of discounts; they would have been able, in all probability, to have continued their payments till the alarm had subsided. At any rate, as the debtors to the Bank would have been obliged to discharge their debts in the space of sixty days, that being the longest period for which any bill discounted by the Bank has to run, the directors would in that time, if necessary, have been enabled to redeem every note in circulation. It was then owing to the too intimate connection between the Bank and government that the restriction became necessary; it is to that cause, too, that we owe its continuance.

To prevent the evil consequences which may attend the perseverance in this system, we must keep our eyes steadily fixed on the repeal of the Restriction-bill.

The only legitimate security which the public can possess against the indiscretion of the Bank is to oblige them to pay their notes on demand in specie; and this can only be effected by diminishing the amount of bank notes in circulation till the nominal price of gold be lowered to the mint price.

Here I will conclude, happy if my feeble efforts should awaken the public attention to a due consideration of the state of our circulating medium. I am well aware that I have not added to the stock of information with which the public has been enlightened by many able writers on the same important subject. I have had no such ambition. My aim has been to introduce a calm and dispassionate inquiry into a question of great importance to the State, and the neglect of which may be attended with consequences which every friend of his country would deplore.

Notes

1. They might, strictly speaking, rather exceed that quantity, because as the Bank would add to the currency of the world, England would retain its share of the increase.

2. This is strongly corroborated, by the statement of Mr. Rose, in the House of Commons, that our exports exceeded our imports by (I believe) sixteen millions. In return for those exports, no bullion could have been imported, because it is well known that the price of bullion having been during the whole year higher abroad than in this country, a large quantity of our gold coin has been exported. To the value of the balance of exports, therefore, must be added the value of the bullion exported. A part of the amount may be due to us from foreign nations, but the reminder must be precisely equal to our foreign expenditure, consisting of subsidies to our allies, and the maintenance of our fleets and armies on foreign stations.

3. It has been observed, in a work of great and deserved repute, the *Edinburgh Review*, that an increase in the paper currency will only occasion a rise in the paper or currency price of commodities, but will not cause an increase in their bullion price.

    This would be true at a time when the currency consisted wholly of paper not convertible into specie, but not while specie formed any part of the circulation. In the latter case the effect of an increased issue of paper would be to throw out of circulation an equal amount of specie; but this could not be done without adding to the quantity of bullion in the market, and thereby lowering its value, or in other words, increasing the bullion price of commodities. It is only in consequence of this fall in the value of the metallic currency, and of bullion, that the temptation to export them arises; and the penalties on melting the coin is the sole cause of a small difference between the value of the coin and of bullion, or a small excess of the market above the mint price. But exporting of bullion is synonymous with an unfavourable balance of trade. From whatever cause an exportation of bullion, in exchange for commodities, may proceed, it is called (I think very incorrectly) an unfavourable balance of trade.

    When the circulation consists wholly of paper, any increase in its quantity will raise the money price of bullion without lowering its value, in the same manner, and in the same proportion, as it will raise the prices of other commodities, and for the same reason will lower the foreign exchanges; but this will only be a nominal, not a real fall, and will not occasion the exportation of bullion, because the real value of bullion will not be diminished, as there will be no increase to the quantity in the market.

4. Strictly speaking, there can be no permanent measure of value. A measure of value should itself be invariable; but this is not the case with either gold or silver, they being subject to fluctuations as well as other commodities. Experience has indeed taught us, that though the variations in the value of gold or silver may be considerable, on a comparison of distant periods, yet for short spaces of time their value is tolerably fixed. It is this property, among their other excellencies, which fits them better than any other commodity for the uses of money. Either gold or silver may therefore, in the point of view in which we are considering them, be called a measure of value.

5. When the gold coin was debased, previously to the re-coinage in 1774, gold and silver bullion rose above their mint prices, and fell immediately on the gold coin attaining its present perfection. The exchanges were, owing to the same causes, from being unfavourable rendered favourable.

6. An excess in the market above the mint price of gold or silver bullion, may, whilst the coins of both metals are legal tender, and there is no prohibition against the coinage of either metal, be caused by a variation in the relative value of those metals; but an excess of the market above the mint price prodding from this cause will be at once perceived by its affecting only the price of one of the metals. Thus gold would be at or below, while silver was above, its mint price, or silver at or below its mint price, whilst gold was above.

In the latter end of 1795, when the Bank had considerably more notes in circulation than either the preceding or the subsequent year, when their embarrassments had already commenced, when they appear to have resigned all prudence in the management of their concerns, and to have constituted Mr. Pitt sole director, the price of gold bullion did for a short time rise to 4l. 3s., or 4l. 4s. per ounce; but the directors were not without their fears for the consequences. In a remonstrance sent by them to Mr. Pitt, dated October 1795, after stating, "that the demand for gold not appearing likely soon to cease," and "that it had excited great apprehension in the court of directors," they observe, "The present price of gold being 4l. 3s. to 4l. 4s. [It is difficult to determine on what authority the directors made this assertion, as by a return lately made to Parliament it appears that during the year 1795 they did not purchase gold bullion at a price higher than 3l. 17s. 6d.] per ounce, and our guineas being to be purchased at 3l. 17s. 10½d., clearly demonstrates the grounds of our fears; it being only necessary to state those facts to the Chancellor of the Exchequer." It is remarkable that no price of gold above the mint price is quoted during the whole year in Wetenhall's list. In December it is there marked 3l. 17s. 6d.

7. The relative value of gold and silver is on the continent nearly the same as in London.

8. It must be meant that every guinea in the Bank would leave the country, the temptation of fifteen per cent is amply sufficient to send those out which can be collected from the circulation.

9. They might, on some occasion, displace Bank of England notes, but that consideration does not affect the question which we are now discussing.

10. In the following observations, I wish it to be understood, as supposing always the same degree of confidence and credit to exist.

11. I have already allowed that the Bank, as far as they enable us to turn our coin into "materials, provisions, etc." have produced a national benefit, as they have thereby increased the quantity of productive capital; but I am here speaking of an excess of their notes, of that quantity which adds to our circulation without effecting any corresponding exportation of coin, and which, therefore, degrades the notes below the value of the bullion contained in the coin which they represent.

12. At that period the price of gold kept steadily under its mint price.

Essays on Political Economy
Part I: Capital and Interest

Frédéric Bastiat; 1848

My object in this treatise is to examine into the real nature of the *Interest of Capital*, for the purpose of proving that it is lawful, and explaining why it should be perpetual. This may appear singular, and yet, I confess, I am more afraid of being too plain than too obscure. I am afraid I may weary the reader by a series of mere truisms. But it is no easy matter to avoid this danger, when the facts with which we have to deal are known to every one by personal, familiar, and daily experience.

But then, you will say, "What is the use of this treatise? Why explain what everybody knows?"

But, although this problem appears at first sight so very simple, there is more in it than you might suppose. I shall endeavor to prove this by an example. "Mondor lends an instrument of labour today, which will be entirely destroyed in a week, yet the capital will not produce the less interest to Mondor or his heirs, through all eternity." Reader, can you honestly say that you understand the reason of this?

It would be a waste of time to seek any satisfactory explanation from the writings of economists. They have not thrown much light upon the reasons of the existence of interest. For this they are not to be blamed; for at the time they wrote, its lawfulness was not called in question. Now, however, times are altered; the case is different. Men, who consider themselves to be in advance of their age, have organized an active crusade against capital and interest; it is the productiveness of capital which they are attacking; not certain abuses in the administration of it, but the principle itself.

A journal has been established to serve as a vehicle for this crusade. It is conducted by M. Proudhon, and has, it is said, an immense circulation. The first number of this periodical contains the electoral manifesto of the *Le Peuple*. Here we read, "The productiveness of capital, which is condemned by Christianity under the name of usury, is the

97

cause of misery, the true principle of destitution, the eternal obstacle to the establishment of the Republic."

Another journal, *La Ruche Populaire*, after having said some excellent things on labour, adds, "But, above all, labour ought to be free; that is, it ought to be organized in such a manner, *that money-lenders and patrons, or masters, should not be paid* for this liberty of labour, this right of labour, which is raised to so high a price by the traffickers of men." The only thought that I notice here, is that expressed by the words in italics, which imply a denial of the right to interest. The remainder of the article explains it.

It is thus that the democratic Socialist, Thoré, expresses himself:

"The revolution will always have to be recommenced, so long as we occupy ourselves with consequences only, without having the logic or the courage to attack the principle itself. This principle is capital, false property, interest, and usury, which by the old régime, is made to weigh upon labour.

"Ever since the aristocrats invented the incredible fiction, that capital possesses the power of reproducing itself, the workers have been at the mercy of the idle.

"At the end of a year, will you find an additional crown in a bag of one hundred shillings? At the end of fourteen years, will your shillings have doubled in your bag?

"Will a work of industry or of skill produce another, at the end of fourteen years?

"Let us begin, then, by demolishing this fatal fiction."

I have quoted the above, merely for the sake of establishing the fact, that many persons consider the productiveness of capital a false, a fatal, and an iniquitous principle. But quotations are superfluous; it is well known that the people attribute their sufferings to what they call *the trafficking in man by man*. In fact, the phrase, *tyranny of capital*, has become proverbial.

I believe there is not a man in the world, who is aware of the whole importance of this question: "Is the interest of capital natural, just, and lawful, and as useful to the payer as to the receiver?"

You answer, No; I answer, Yes. Then we differ entirely; but it is of the utmost importance to discover which of us is in the right, otherwise we shall incur the danger of making a false solution of the question, a matter of opinion. If the error is on my side, however, the evil would not be so great. It must be inferred that I know nothing about the true interests of the masses, or the march of human progress; and that all my arguments are but as so many grains of sand, by which the car of the revolution will certainly not be arrested.

But if, on the contrary, MM. Proudhon and Thoré are deceiving themselves, it follows that they are leading the people astray—that they are showing them the evil where it does not exist; and thus giving a false direction to their ideas, to their antipathies, to their dislikes, and to their attacks. It follows that the misguided people are rushing into a horrible and absurd struggle, in which victory would be more fatal than defeat; since, according to this supposition, the result would be the realization of universal evils, the destruction of every means of emancipation, the consummation of its own misery.

This is just what M. Proudhon has acknowledged, with perfect good faith. "The foundation stone," he told me, "of my system is the *gratuitousness of credit*. If I am mistaken in this, Socialism is a vain dream." I add, it is a dream, in which the people are tearing themselves to pieces. Will it, therefore, be a cause for surprise, if, when they awake, they find themselves mangled and bleeding? Such a danger as this is enough to justify me fully, if, in the course of the discussion, I allow myself to be led into some trivialities and some prolixity.

Capital and Interest

I address this treatise to the workmen of Paris, more especially to those who have enrolled themselves under the banner of Socialist democracy. I proceed to consider these two questions:

1st. Is it consistent with the nature of things, and with justice, that capital should produce interest?

2nd. Is it consistent with the nature of things, and with justice, that the interest of capital should be perpetual?

The working men of Paris will certainly acknowledge that a more important subject could not be discussed.

Since the world began, it has been allowed, at least in part, that capital ought to produce interest. But latterly it has been affirmed, that herein lies the very social error which is the cause of pauperism and inequality. It is, therefore, very essential to know now on what ground we stand.

For if levying interest from capital is a sin, the workers have a right to revolt against social order, as it exists. It is in vain to tell them that they ought to have recourse to legal and pacific means, it would be a hypocritical recommendation. When on the one side there is a strong man, poor, and a victim of robbery—on the other, a weak man, but rich, and a robber—it is singular enough that we should say to the former, with a hope of persuading him, "Wait till your oppressor voluntarily renounces oppression, or till it shall cease of itself." This cannot be; and those who tell us that capital is by nature unproductive, ought to know that they are provoking a terrible and immediate struggle.

If, on the contrary, the interest of capital is natural, lawful, con- sistent with the general good, as favourable to the borrower as to the lender, the economists who deny it, the tribunes who traffic in this pretended social wound, are leading the workmen into a senseless and unjust struggle, which can have no other issue than the misfortune of all. In fact, they are arming labour against capital. So much the better, if these two powers are really antagonistic; and may the struggle soon be ended! But if they are in harmony, the struggle is the greatest evil which can be inflicted on society. You see, then, workmen, that there is not a more important question than this: "Is the interest of capital lawful or not?" In the former case, you must immediately renounce the struggle to which you are being urged; in the second, you must carry it on brav- ely, and to the end.

Productiveness of capital; perpetuity of interest. These are difficult questions. I must endeavor to make myself clear. And for that purpose I shall have recourse to example rather than to demonstration; or rather, I shall place the demonstration in the example. I begin by ac- knowledging that, at first sight, it may appear strange that capital should pretend to a remuneration, and above all, to a perpetual re- muneration. You will say, "Here are two men. One of them works from morning till night, from one year's end to another; and if he consumes all which he has gained, even by superior energy, he remains poor. When Christmas comes he is no forwarder than he was at the beginning of the year, and has no other prospect but to begin again. The other man does nothing, either with his hands or his head; or at least, if he makes use of them at all, it is only for his own pleasure; it is allowable for him to do nothing, for he has an income. He does not work, yet he lives well; he has everything in abundance; delicate dishes, sumptuous furniture, elegant equipages; nay, he even consumes, daily, things which the workers have been obliged to produce by the sweat of their brow, for these things do not make themselves; and, as far as he is concerned, he has had no hand in their production. It is the workmen who have caused this corn to grow, polished this furniture, woven these carpets; it is our wives and daughters who have spun, cut out, sewed, and embroidered these stuffs. We work, then, for him and for our-selves; for him first, and then for ourselves, if there is anything left. But here is something more striking still. If the former of these two men, the worker, consumes within the year any profit which may have been left him in that year, he is always at the point from which he started, and his destiny condemns him to move incessantly in a perpetual circle, and a monotony of exertion. Labour, then, is rewarded only once. But if the other, the 'gentleman,' consumes his yearly income in the year, he has, the year after, in those which follow, and through all eternity, an in-come always equal, inexhaustible, *perpetual*. Capital, then, is remu-nerated, not only once or twice, but an indefinite number of times! So that, at the end of a hundred years, a family which has placed twenty thousand francs, at five per cent, will have had one hundred thousand francs; and this will not prevent it from having one hundred thousand more, in the following century. In other words, for twenty thousand francs, which represent its labour, it will have levied, in two centuries, a tenfold value on the labour of others. In this social arrangement, is there not a monstrous evil to be reformed? And this is not all. If it should please this family to curtail its enjoyments a little—to spend, for example, only nine hundred francs, instead of one thousand—it may, without any labour, without any other trouble beyond that of investing one hundred francs a year, increase its capital and its income in such ra-pid progression, that it will soon be in a position to consume as much as a hundred families of industrious workmen. Does not all this go to prove that society itself has in its bosom a hideous cancer, which ought to be eradicated at the risk of some temporary suffering?"

These are, it appears to me, the sad and irritating reflections which must be excited in your minds by the active and superficial crusade which is being carried on against capital and interest. On the other hand, there are moments in which, I am convinced, doubts are awakened in your minds, and scruples in your conscience. You say to yourselves sometimes, "But to assert that capital ought not to produce interest, is to say that he who has created instruments of labour, or materials, or provisions of any kind, ought to yield them up without compensation. Is that just? And then, if it is so, who would lend these instruments, these materials, these provisions? Who would take care of them? Who even would create them? Every one would consume his proportion, and the human race would never advance a step. Capital would be no longer formed, since there would be no interest in forming it. It would become exceedingly scarce. A singular step towards gratuitous loans! A singular means of improving the condition of borrowers, to make it impossible for them to borrow at any price! What would become of labour itself? For there will be no money advanced, and not one single kind of labour can be mentioned, not even the chase, which can be pursued without money in hand. And, as for ourselves, what would become of us? What! We are not to be allowed to borrow, in order to work in the prime of life, nor to lend, that we may enjoy repose in its decline? The law will rob us of the prospect of laying by a little property, because it will prevent us from gaining any advantage from it. It will deprive us of all stimulus to save at the present time, and of all hope of repose for the future. It is useless to exhaust ourselves with fatigue; we must abandon the idea of leaving our sons and daughters a little property, since modern science renders it useless, for we should become traffickers in men if we were to lend it on interest. Alas, the world which these persons would open before us, as an imaginary good, is still more dreary and desolate than that which they condemn, for hope, at any rate, is not banished from the latter." Thus, in all respects, and in every point of view, the question is a serious one. Let us hasten to arrive at a solution.

Our civil code has a chapter entitled, "On the manner of transmitting property." I do not think it gives a very complete nomenclature on this point. When a man by his labour has made some useful thing—in other words, when he has created a *value*—it can only pass into the hands of another by one of the following modes: as a gift, by the right of inheritance, by exchange, loan, or theft. One word upon each of these, except the last, although it plays a greater part in the world than we may think.

A gift needs no definition. It is essentially voluntary and spontaneous. It depends exclusively upon the giver, and the receiver cannot be said to have any right to it. Without a doubt, morality and religion make it a duty for men, especially the rich, to deprive themselves voluntarily of that which they possess, in favour of their less fortunate brethren. But this is an entirely moral obligation. If it were to be asserted on principle, admitted in practice, or sanctioned by law, that every man has a right to the property of another, the gift would have no merit—charity and gratitude would be no longer virtues. Besides, such a doctrine would suddenly and universally arrest labour and production, as severe cold congeals water and suspends animation; for who would work if there was no longer to be any connection between labour and the satisfying of our wants? Political economy has not treated of gifts. It has hence been concluded that it disowns them, and that it is therefore a science devoid of heart. This is a ridiculous accusation. That science which treats of the laws resulting from the *reciprocity of services*, had no business to inquire into the consequences of generosity with respect to him who receives, nor into its effects, perhaps still more precious, on him who gives; such considerations belong evidently to the science of morals. We must allow the sciences to have limits; above all, we must not accuse them of denying or undervaluing what they look upon as foreign to their department.

The right of inheritance, against which so much has been objected of late, is one of the forms of gift, and assuredly the most natural of all. That which a man has produced, he may consume, exchange, or give. What can be more natural than that he should give it to his children? It is this power, more than any other, which inspires him with courage to labour and to save. Do you know why the principle of right of inheritance is thus called in question? Because it is imagined that the property thus transmitted is plundered from the masses. This is a fatal error. Political economy demonstrates, in the most peremptory manner, that all value produced is a creation which does no harm to any person whatever. For that reason it may be consumed, and, still more, transmitted, without hurting any one; but I shall not pursue these reflections, which do not belong to the subject.

Exchange is the principal department of political economy, because it is by far the most frequent method of transmitting property, according to the free and voluntary agreements of the laws and effects of which this science treats.

Properly speaking, exchange is the reciprocity of services. The parties say between themselves, "Give me this, and I will give you that;" or, "Do this for me, and I will do that for you." It is well to remark (for this will throw a new light on the notion of value), that the second form is always implied in the first. When it is said, "Do this for me, and I will do that for you," an exchange of service for service is proposed. Again, when it is said, "Give me this, and I will give you that," it is the same as saying, "I yield to you what I have done, yield to me what you have done." The labour is past, instead of present; but the exchange is not the less governed by the comparative valuation of the two services; so that it is quite correct to say that the principle of *value* is in the services rendered and received on account of the productions exchanged, rather than in the productions themselves.

In reality, services are scarcely ever exchanged directly. There is a medium, which is termed *money*. Paul has completed a coat, for which he wishes to receive a little bread, a little wine, a little oil, a visit from a doctor, a ticket for the play, etc. The exchange cannot be effected in kind, so what does Paul do? He first exchanges his coat for some money, which is called *sale*; then he exchanges this money again for the things which he wants, which is called *purchase*; and now, only, has the reciprocity of services completed its circuit; now, only, the labour and the compensation are balanced in the same individual,—"I have done this for society, it has done that for me." In a word, it is only now that the exchange is actually accomplished. Thus, nothing can be more correct than this observation of J.B. Say: "Since the introduction of money, every exchange is resolved into two elements, *sale* and *purchase*. It is the reunion of these two elements which renders the exchange complete."

We must remark, also, that the constant appearance of money in every exchange has overturned and misled all our ideas; men have ended in thinking that money was true riches, and that to multiply it was to multiply services and products. Hence the prohibitory system; hence paper money; hence the celebrated aphorism, "What one gains the other loses;" and all the errors which have ruined the earth, and imbrued it with blood.[1] After much research it has been found, that in order to make the two services exchanged of equivalent value, and in order to render the exchange *equitable*, the best means was to allow it to be free. However plausible, at first sight, the intervention of the State might be, it was soon perceived that it is always oppressive to one or other of the contracting parties. When we look into these subjects, we are always compelled to reason upon this maxim, that *equal value* results from liberty. We have, in fact, no other means of knowing whether, at a given moment, two services are of the same value, but that of examining whether they can be readily and freely exchanged. Allow the State, which is the same thing as force, to interfere on one side or the other, and from that moment all the means of appreciation will be complicated and entangled, instead of becoming clear. It ought to be the part of the State to prevent, and, above all, to repress artifice and fraud; that is, to secure liberty, and not to violate it. I have enlarged a little upon exchange, although loan is my principal object: My excuse is, that I conceive that there is in a loan an actual exchange, an actual service rendered by the lender, and which makes the borrower liable to an equivalent service,—two services, whose comparative value can only be appreciated, like that of all possible services, by freedom. Now, if it is so, the perfect lawfulness of what is called house rent, farm rent, interest, will be explained and justified. Let us consider the case of *loan*.

Suppose two men exchange two services or two objects, whose equal value is beyond all dispute. Suppose, for example, Peter says to Paul, "Give me ten sixpences, I will give you a five-shilling piece." We cannot imagine an equal value more unquestionable. When the bargain is made, neither party has any claim upon the other. The exchanged services are equal. Thus it follows, that if one of the parties wishes to introduce into the bargain an additional clause, advantageous to himself, but unfavourable to the other party, he must agree to a second clause, which shall re-establish the equilibrium, and the law of justice. It would be absurd to deny the justice of a second clause of compensation. This granted, we will suppose that Peter, after having said to Paul, "Give me ten sixpences, I will give you a crown," adds, "You shall give me the ten sixpences *now*, and I will give you the crown-piece *in a year*;" it is very evident that this new proposition alters the claims and advantages of the bargain; that it alters the proportion of the two services. Does it not appear plainly enough, in fact, that Peter asks of Paul a new and an additional service; one of a different kind? Is it not as if he had said, "Render me the service of allowing me to use for my profit, for a year, five shillings which belong to you, and which you might have used for yourself?" And what good reason have you to maintain that Paul is bound to render this especial service gratuitously; that he has no right to demand anything more in consequence of this requisition; that the State ought to interfere to force him to submit? Is it not incomprehensible that the economist, who preaches such a doctrine to the people, can reconcile it with his principle of *the reciprocity of services*? Here I have introduced cash; I have been led to do so by a desire to place, side by side, two objects of exchange, of a perfect and indisputable equality of value. I was anxious to be prepared for objections; but, on the other hand, my demonstration would have been more striking still, if I had illustrated my principle by an agreement for exchanging the services or the productions themselves.

Suppose, for example, a house and a vessel of a value so perfectly equal that their proprietors are disposed to exchange them evenhanded, without excess or abatement. In fact let the bargain be settled by a lawyer. At the moment of each taking possession, the ship-owner says to the citizen, "Very well; the transaction is completed, and nothing can prove its perfect equity better than our free and voluntary consent. Our conditions thus fixed, I shall propose to you a little practical modification. You shall let me have your house today, but I shall not put you in possession of my ship for a year; and the reason I make this demand of you is, that, during this year of *delay*, I wish to use the vessel." That we may not be embarrassed by considerations relative to the deterioration of the thing lent, I will suppose the ship-owner to add, "I will engage, at the end of the year, to hand over to you the vessel in the state in which it is today." I ask of every candid man, I ask of M. Proudhon himself, if the citizen has not a right to answer, "The new clause which you propose entirely alters the proportion or the equal value of the exchanged services. By it, I shall be deprived, for the space of a year, both at once of my house and of your vessel. By it, you will make use of both. If, in the absence of this clause, the bargain was just, for the same reason the clause is injurious to me. It stipulates for a loss to me, and a gain to you. You are requiring of me a new service; I have a right to refuse, or to require of you, as a compensation, an equivalent service." If the parties are agreed upon this compensation, the principle of which is incontestable, we can easily distinguish two transactions in one, two exchanges of service in one. First, there is the exchange of the house for the vessel; after this, there is the delay granted by one of the parties, and the compensation correspondent to this delay yielded by the other. These two new services take the generic and abstract names of *credit* and *interest*. But names do not change the nature of things; and I defy any one to dare to maintain that there exists here, when all is done, a service for a service, or a reciprocity of services. To say that one of these services does not challenge the other, to say that the first ought to be rendered gratuitously, without injustice, is to say that injustice consists in the reciprocity of services,—that justice consists in one of the parties giving and not receiving, which is a contradiction in terms.

To give an idea of interest and its mechanism, allow me to make use of two or three anecdotes. But, first, I must say a few words upon capital.

There are some persons who imagine that capital is money, and this is precisely the reason why they deny its productiveness; for, as M. Thoré says, crowns are not endowed with the power of reproducing themselves. But it is not true that capital and money are the same thing. Before the discovery of the precious metals, there were capitalists in the world; and I venture to say that at that time, as now, everybody was a capitalist, to a certain extent.

What is capital, then? It is composed of three things:

1st. Of the materials upon which men operate, when these materials have already a value communicated by some human effort, which has bestowed upon them the principle of remuneration,—wool, flax, leather, silk, wood, etc.

2nd. Instruments which are used for working,—tools, machines, ships, carriages, etc.

3rd. Provisions which are consumed during labour; victuals, stuffs, houses, etc.

Without these things the labour of man would be unproductive and almost void; yet these very things have required much work, especially at first. This is the reason that so much value has been attached to the possession of them, and also that it is perfectly lawful to exchange and to sell them, to make a profit of them if used, to gain remuneration from them if lent.

Now for my anecdotes.

The Sack of Corn

Mathurin, in other respects as poor as Job, and obliged to earn his bread by day-labour, became, nevertheless, by some inheritance, the owner of a fine piece of uncultivated land. He was exceedingly anxious to cultivate it. "Alas!" said he, "to make ditches, to raise fences, to break the soil, to clear away the brambles and stones, to plough it, to sow it, might bring me a living in a year or two; but certainly not today, or tomorrow. It is impossible to set about farming it, without previously saving some provisions for my subsistence until the harvest; and I know, by experience, that preparatory labour is indispensable, in order to render present labour productive." The good Mathurin was not content with making these reflections. He resolved to work by the day, and to save something from his wages to buy a spade and a sack of corn; without which things, he must give up his fine agricultural projects. He acted so well, was so active and steady, that he soon saw himself in possession of the wished-for sack of corn. "I shall take it to the mill," said he, "and then I shall have enough to live upon till my field is covered with a rich harvest." Just as he was starting, Jerome came to borrow his treasure of him. "If you will lend me this sack of corn," said Jerome, "you will do me a great service; for I have some very lucrative work in view, which I cannot possibly undertake, for want of provisions to live upon until it is finished." "I was in the same case," answered Mathurin, "and if I have now secured bread for several months, it is at the expense of my arms and my stomach. Upon what principle of justice can it be devoted to the realization of *your* enterprise instead of *mine?*"

You may well believe that the bargain was a long one. However, it was finished at length, and on these conditions:

First, Jerome promised to give back, at the end of the year, a sack of corn of the same quality, and of the same weight, without missing a single grain. "This first clause is perfectly just," said he, "for without it Mathurin would *give*, and not *lend*."

Secondly, He engaged to deliver *five litres on every hectolitre*. "This clause is no less just than the other," thought he; "for without it Mathurin would do me a service without compensation; he would inflict upon himself a privation—he would renounce his cherished enterprise—he would cause me to enjoy for a year the fruits of his savings, and all this gratuitously. Since he delays the cultivation of his land, since he enables me to realize a lucrative labour, it is quite natural that I should let him partake, in a certain proportion, of the profits which I shall gain by the sacrifice he makes of his own."

On his side, Mathurin, who was something of a scholar, made this calculation: "Since, by virtue of the first clause, the sack of corn will return to me at the end of a year," he said to himself, "I shall be able to lend it again; it will return to me at the end of the second year; I may lend it again, and so on, to all eternity. However, I cannot deny that it will have been eaten long ago. It is singular that I should be perpetually the owner of a sack of corn, although the one I have lent has been consumed for ever. But this is explained thus: It will be consumed in the service of Jerome. It will put it into the power of Jerome to produce a superior value; and, consequently, Jerome will be able to restore me a sack of corn, or the value of it, without having suffered the slightest injury: but quite the contrary. And as regards myself, this value ought to be my property, as long as I do not consume it myself. If I had used it to clear my land, I should have received it again in the form of a fine harvest. Instead of that, I lend it, and shall recover it in the form of repayment.

"From the second clause, I gain another piece of information. At the end of the year I shall be in possession of five litres of corn over the one hundred that I have just lent. If, then, I were to continue to work by the day, and to save part of my wages, as I have been doing, in the course of time I should be able to lend two sacks of corn; then three; then four; and when I should have gained a sufficient number to enable me to live on these additions of five litres over and above each, I shall be at liberty to take a little repose in my old age. But how is this? In this case, shall I not be living at the expense of others? No, certainly, for it has been proved that in lending I perform a service; I complete the labour of my borrowers, and only deduct a trifling part of the excess of production, due to my lendings and savings. It is a marvelous thing that a man may thus realize a leisure which injures no one, and for which he cannot be envied without injustice."

The House

Mondor had a house. In building it, he had extorted nothing from any one whatever. He owed it to his own personal labour, or, which is the same thing, to labour justly rewarded. His first care was to make a bargain with an architect, in virtue of which, by means of a hundred crowns a year, the latter engaged to keep the house in constant good repair. Mondor was already congratulating himself on the happy days which he hoped to spend in this retreat, declared sacred by our Constitution. But Valerius wished to make it his residence.

"How can you think of such a thing?" said Mondor to Valerius. "It is I who have built it; it has cost me ten years of painful labour, and now you would enjoy it!" They agreed to refer the matter to judges. They chose no profound economists,—there were none such in the country. But they found some just and sensible men; it all comes to the same thing; political economy, justice, good sense, are all the same thing. Now here is the decision made by the judges: If Valerius wishes to occupy Mondor's house for a year, he is bound to submit to three conditions. The first is to quit at the end of the year, and to restore the house in good repair, saving the inevitable decay resulting from mere duration. The second, to refund to Mondor the three hundred francs which the latter pays annually to the architect to repair the injuries of time; for these injuries taking place whilst the house is in the service of Valerius, it is perfectly just that he should bear the consequences. The third, that he should render to Mondor a service equivalent to that which he receives. As to this equivalence of services, it must be freely discussed between Mondor and Valerius.

The Plane

A very long time ago there lived, in a poor village, a joiner, who was a philosopher, as all my heroes are in their way. James worked from morning till night with his two strong arms, but his brain was not idle for all that. He was fond of reviewing his actions, their causes, and their effects. He sometimes said to himself, "With my hatchet, my saw, and my hammer, I can make only coarse furniture, and can only get the pay for such. If I only had a *plane*, I should please my customers more, and they would pay me more. It is quite just; I can only expect services proportioned to those which I render myself. Yes! I am resolved, I will make myself a *plane*."

However, just as he was setting to work, James reflected further: "I work for my customers three hundred days in the year. If I give ten to making my plane, supposing it lasts me a year, only two hundred and ninety days will remain for me to make my furniture. Now, in order that I be not the loser in this matter, I must gain henceforth, with the help of the plane, as much in two hundred and ninety days, as I now do in three hundred. I must even gain more; for unless I do so, it would not be worth my while to venture upon any innovations." James began to calculate. He satisfied himself that he should sell his finished furniture at a price which would amply compensate for the ten days devoted to the plane; and when no doubt remained on this point, he set to work. I beg the reader to remark, that the power which exists in the tool to increase the productiveness of labour, is the basis of the solution which follows.

At the end of ten days, James had in his possession an admirable plane, which he valued all the more for having made it himself. He danced for joy,—for, like the girl with her basket of eggs, he reckoned all the profits which he expected to derive from the ingenious instrument; but, more fortunate than she, he was not reduced to the necessity of saying good-bye to calf, cow, pig, and eggs, together. He was building his fine castles in the air, when he was interrupted by his acquaintance William, a joiner in the neighbouring village. William having admired the plane, was struck with the advantages which might be gained from it. He said to James:

W. You must do me a service.

J. What service?

W. Lend me the plane for a year.

As might be expected, James at this proposal did not fail to cry out, "How can you think of such a thing, William? Well, if I do you this service, what will you do for me in return?"

W. Nothing. Don't you know that a loan ought to be gratuitous? Don't you know that capital is naturally unproductive? Don't you know fraternity has been proclaimed. If you only do me a service for the sake of receiving one from me in return, what merit would you have?

J. William, my friend, fraternity does not mean that all the sacrifices are to be on one side; if so, I do not see why they should not be on yours. Whether a loan should be gratuitous I don't know; but I do know that if I were to lend you my plane for a year it would be giving it you. To tell you the truth, that was not what I made it for.

W. Well, we will say nothing about the modern maxims discovered by the Socialist gentlemen. I ask you to do me a service; what service do you ask me in return?

J. First, then, in a year, the plane will be done for, it will be good for nothing. It is only just, that you should let me have another exactly like it; or that you should give me money enough to get it repaired; or that you should supply me the ten days which I must devote to replacing it.

W. This is perfectly just. I submit to these conditions. I engage to return it, or to let you have one like it, or the value of the same. I think you must be satisfied with this, and can require nothing further.

J. I think otherwise. I made the plane for myself, and not for you. I expected to gain some advantage from it, by my work being better finished and better paid, by an improvement in my condition. What reason is there that I should make the plane, and you should gain the profit? I might as well ask you to give me your saw and hatchet! What a confusion! Is it not natural that each should keep what he has made with his own hands, as well as his hands themselves? To use without recompense the hands of another, I call slavery; to use without recompense the plane of another, can this be called fraternity?

W. But, then, I have agreed to return it to you at the end of a year, as well polished and as sharp as it is now.

J. We have nothing to do with next year; we are speaking of this year. I have made the plane for the sake of improving my work and condition; if you merely return it to me in a year, it is you who will gain the profit of it during the whole of that time. I am not bound to do you such a service without receiving anything from you in return: therefore, if you wish for my plane, independently of the entire restoration already bargained for, you must do me a service which we will now discuss; you must grant me remuneration.

And this was done thus: William granted a remuneration calculated in such a way that, at the end of the year, James received his plane quite new, and in addition, a compensation, consisting of a new plank, for the advantages of which he had deprived himself, and which he had yielded to his friend.

It was impossible for anyone acquainted with the transaction to discover the slightest trace in it of oppression or injustice.

The singular part of it is, that, at the end of the year, the plane came into James' possession, and he lent it again; recovered it, and lent it a third and fourth time. It has passed into the hands of his son, who still lends it. Poor plane! how many times has it changed, sometimes its blade, sometimes its handle. It is no longer the same plane, but it has always the same value, at least for James' posterity. Workmen! Let us examine into these little stories.

I maintain, first of all, that the *sack of corn* and the *plane* are here the type, the model, a faithful representation, the symbol of all capital; as the five litres of corn and the plank are the type, the model, the representation, the symbol of all interest. This granted, the following are, it seems to me, a series of consequences, the justice of which it is impossible to dispute.

1st. If the yielding of a plank by the borrower to the lender is a natural, equitable, lawful remuneration, the just price of a real service, we may conclude that, as a general rule, it is in the nature of capital to produce interest. When this capital, as in the foregoing examples, takes the form of an *instrument of labour*, it is clear enough that it ought to bring an advantage to its possessor, to him who has devoted to it his time, his brains, and his strength. Otherwise, why should he have made it? No necessity of life can be immediately satisfied with instruments of labour; no one eats planes or drinks saws, except, indeed, he be a con-juror. If a man determines to spend his time in the production of such things, he must have been led to it by the consideration of the power which these instruments add to his power; of the time which they save him; of the perfection and rapidity which they give to his labour; in a word, of the advantages which they procure for him. Now, these advantages, which have been prepared by labour, by the sacrifice of time which might have been used in a more immediate manner, are we

bound, as soon as they are ready to be enjoyed, to confer them gratuitously upon another? Would it be an advance in social order, if the
law decided thus, and citizens should pay officials for causing such a law
to be executed by force? I venture to say, that there is not one amongst
you who would support it. It would be to legalize, to organize, to sys-
tematize injustice itself, for it would be proclaiming that there are men
born to render, and others born to receive, gratuitous services. Granted,
then, that interest is just, natural, and lawful.

2nd. A second consequence, not less remarkable than the former,
and, if possible, still more conclusive, to which I call your attention, is
this: *Interest is not injurious to the borrower*. I mean to say, the obligation in which the borrower finds himself, to pay a remuneration for
the use of capital, cannot do any harm to his condition. Observe, in fact,
that James and William are perfectly free, as regards the transaction to
which the plane gave occasion. The transaction cannot be accomplished
without the consent of the one as well as of the other. The worst which
can happen is, that James may be too exacting; and in this case, William,
refusing the loan, remains as he was before. By the fact of his agreeing
to borrow, he proves that he considers it an advantage to himself; he
proves, that after every calculation, including the remuneration, whatever it may be, required of him, he still finds it more profitable to
borrow than not to borrow. He only determines to do so because he has
compared the inconveniences with the advantages. He has calculated
that the day on which he returns the plane, accompanied by the
remuneration agreed upon, he will have effected more work, with the
same labour, thanks to this tool. A profit will remain to him, otherwise
he would not have borrowed. The two services of which we are
speaking are exchanged according to the law which governs all
exchanges, the law of supply and demand. The claims of James have a
natural and impassable limit. This is the point in which the remuneration demanded by him would absorb all the advantage which William
might find in making use of a plane. In this case, the borrowing would
not take place. William would be bound either to make a plane for
himself, or to do without one, which would leave him in his original
condition. He borrows, because he gains by borrowing. I know very well
what will be told me. You will say, William may be deceived, or, perhaps, he may be governed by necessity, and be obliged to submit to a
harsh law.

It may be so. As to errors in calculation, they belong to the infirmity
of our nature, and to argue from this against the transaction in

question, is objecting the possibility of loss in all imaginable trans-actions, in every human act. Error is an accidental fact, which is inces-santly remedied by experience. In short, everybody must guard against it. As far as those hard necessities are concerned, which force persons to burdensome borrowings, it is clear that these necessities exist pre-viously to the borrowing. If William is in a situation in which he cannot possibly do without a plane, and must borrow one at any price, does this situation result from James having taken the trouble to make the tool? Does it not exist independently of this circumstance? However harsh, however severe James may be, he will never render the supposed condition of William worse than it is. Morally, it is true, the lender will be to blame; but, in an economical point of view, the loan itself can never be considered responsible for previous necessities, which it has not created, and which it relieves to a certain extent.

But this proves something to which I shall return. The evident interests of William, representing here the borrowers, there are many Jameses and planes, in other words, lenders and capitals. It is very evident, that if William can say to James,—"Your demands are exor-bitant; there is no lack of planes in the world;" he will be in a better situation than if James' plane was the only one to be borrowed. As-suredly, there is no maxim more true than this—service for service. But let us not forget that no service has a fixed and absolute value, compared with others. The contracting parties are free. Each carries his requisitions to the farthest possible point, and the most favourable circumstance for these requisitions is the absence of rivalship. Hence it follows, that if there is a class of men more interested than any other in the formation, multiplication, and abundance of capitals, it is mainly that of the borrowers. Now, since capitals can only be formed and in-creased by the stimulus and the prospect of remuneration, let this class understand the injury they are inflicting on themselves when they deny the lawfulness of interest, when they proclaim that credit should be gratuitous, when they declaim against the pretended tyranny of capital, when they discourage saving, thus forcing capitals to become scarce, and consequently interests to rise.

3rd. The anecdote I have just related enables you to explain this apparently singular phenomenon, which is termed the duration or per-petuity of interest. Since, in lending his plane, James has been able, very lawfully, to make it a condition that it should be returned to him, at the end of a year, in the same state in which it was when he lent it, is it not evident that he may, at the expiration of the term, lend it again on the same conditions? If he resolves upon the latter plan, the plane will return to him at the end of every year, and that without end. James will then be in a condition to lend it without end; that is, he may derive from it a perpetual interest. It will be said, that the plane will be worn out. That is true; but it will be worn out by the hand and for the profit of the borrower. The latter has taken into account this gradual wear, and taken upon himself, as he ought, the consequences. He has reckoned that he shall derive from this tool an advantage, which will allow him to restore it in its original condition, after having realized a profit from it. As long as James does not use this capital himself, or for his own advantage—as long as he renounces the advantages which allow it to be restored to its original condition—he will have an incontestable right to have it restored, and that independently of interest.

Observe, besides, that if, as I believe I have shown, James, far from doing any harm to William, has done him a *service* in lending him his plane for a year; for the same reason, he will do no harm to a second, a third, a fourth borrower, in the subsequent periods. Hence you may understand that the interest of a capital is as natural, as lawful, as useful, in the thousandth year, as in the first. We may go still further. It may happen that James lends more than a single plane. It is possible, that by means of working, of saving, of privations, of order, of activity, he may come to lend a multitude of planes and saws; that is to say, to do a multitude of services. I insist upon this point,—that if the first loan has been a social good, it will be the same with all the others; for they are all similar, and based upon the same principle. It may happen, then, that the amount of all the remunerations received by our honest operative, in exchange for services rendered by him, may suffice to maintain him. In this case, there will be a man in the world who has a right to live without working. I do not say that he would be doing right to give himself up to idleness,—but I say, that he has a right to do so; and if he does so, it will be at nobody's expense, but quite the contrary. If society at all understands the nature of things, it will acknowledge that this man subsists on services which he receives certainly (as we all do), but which he lawfully receives in exchange for other services, which he himself has rendered, that he continues to render, and which are quite real, inasmuch as they are freely and voluntarily accepted.

And here we have a glimpse of one of the finest harmonies in the social world. I allude to *leisure:* Not that leisure that the warlike and tyrannical classes arrange for themselves by the plunder of the workers, but that leisure which is the lawful and innocent fruit of past activity and economy. In expressing myself thus, I know that I shall shock many received ideas. But see! Is not leisure an essential spring in the social machine? Without it, the world would never have had a Newton, a Pascal, a Fenelon; mankind would have been ignorant of all arts, sciences, and of those wonderful inventions prepared originally by investigations of mere curiosity; thought would have been inert—man would have made no progress. On the other hand, if leisure could only be explained by plunder and oppression—if it were a benefit which could only be enjoyed unjustly, and at the expense of others, there would be no middle path between these two evils; either mankind would be reduced to the necessity of stagnating in a vegetable and stationary life, in eternal ignorance, from the absence of wheels to its machine—or else it would have to acquire these wheels at the price of inevitable injustice, and would necessarily present the sad spectacle, in one form or other, of the antique classification of human beings into masters and slaves. I defy any one to show me, in this case, any other alternative. We should be compelled to contemplate the Divine plan which governs society, with the regret of thinking that it presents a deplorable chasm. The stimulus of progress would be forgotten, or, which is worse, this stimulus would be no other than injustice itself. But, no! God has not left such a chasm in His work of love. We must take care not to disregard His wisdom and power; for those whose imperfect meditations cannot explain the lawfulness of leisure, are very much like the astronomer who said, at a certain point in the heavens there ought to exist a planet which will be at last discovered, for without it the celestial world is not harmony, but discord.

Well, I say that, if well understood, the history of my humble plane, although very modest, is sufficient to raise us to the contemplation of one of the most consoling, but least understood of the social harmonies.

It is not true that we must choose between the denial or the unlawfulness of leisure; thanks to rent and its natural duration, leisure may arise from labour and saving. It is a pleasing prospect, which every one may have in view; a noble recompense, to which each may aspire. It makes its appearance in the world; it distributes itself proportionably to the exercise of certain virtues; it opens all the avenues to intelligence; it ennobles, it raises the morals; it spiritualizes the soul of humanity, not only without laying any weight on those of our brethren whose lot in life devotes them to severe labour, but relieving them gradually from the heaviest and most repugnant part of this labour. It is enough that capitals should be formed, accumulated, multiplied; should be lent on conditions less and less burdensome; that they should descend, penetrate into every social circle, and that by an admirable progression, after having liberated the lenders, they should hasten the liberation of the borrowers themselves. For that end, the laws and customs ought all to be favourable to economy, the source of capital. It is enough to say, that the first of all these conditions is, not to alarm, to attack, to deny that which is the stimulus of saving and the reason of its existence—interest.

As long as we see nothing passing from hand to hand, in the character of loan, but *provisions*, *materials*, *instruments*, things indispensable to the productiveness of labour itself, the ideas thus far exhibited will not find many opponents. Who knows, even, that I may not be reproached for having made a great effort to burst what may be said to be an open door. But as soon as *cash* makes its appearance as the subject of the transaction (and it is this which appears almost always), immediately a crowd of objections are raised. Money, it will be said, will not reproduce itself, like your *sack of corn*; it does not assist labour, like your *plane*; it does not afford an immediate satisfaction, like your *house*. It is incapable, by its nature, of producing interest, of multiplying itself, and the remuneration it demands is a positive extortion.

Who cannot see the sophistry of this? Who does not see that cash is only a transient form, which men give at the time to other *values*, to real objects of usefulness, for the sole object of facilitating their arrangements? In the midst of social complications, the man who is in a condition to lend, scarcely ever has the exact thing which the borrower wants. James, it is true, has a plane; but, perhaps, William wants a saw. They cannot negotiate; the transaction favourable to both cannot take place, and then what happens? It happens that James first exchanges his plane for money; he lends the money to William, and William exchanges the money for a saw. The transaction is no longer a simple one; it is decomposed into two parts, as I explained above in speaking of exchange. But, for all that, it has not changed its nature; it still contains all the elements of a direct loan. James has still got rid of a tool which was useful to him; William has still received an instrument which perfects his work and increases his profits; there is still a service rendered by the lender, which entitles him to receive an equivalent service from the borrower; this just balance is not the less established by free mutual bargaining. The very natural obligation to restore at the end of the term the entire *value*, still constitutes the principle of the duration of interest.

At the end of a year, says M. Thoré, will you find an additional crown in a bag of a hundred pounds?

No, certainly, if the borrower puts the bag of one hundred pounds on the shelf. In such a case, neither the plane nor the sack of corn would reproduce themselves. But it is not for the sake of leaving the money in the bag, nor the plane on the hook, that they are borrowed. The plane is borrowed to be used, or the money to procure a plane. And if it is clearly proved that this tool enables the borrower to obtain profits which he would not have made without it, if it is proved that the lender has renounced creating for himself this excess of profits, we may understand how the stipulation of a part of this excess of profits in favour of the lender, is equitable and lawful.

Ignorance of the true part which cash plays in human transactions, is the source of the most fatal errors. I intend devoting an entire pamphlet to this subject. From what we may infer from the writings of M. Proudhon, that which has led him to think that gratuitous credit was a logical and definite consequence of social progress, is the observation of the phenomenon which shows a decreasing interest, almost in direct proportion to the rate of civilization. In barbarous times it is, in fact, cent, per cent, and more. Then it descends to eighty, sixty, fifty, forty, twenty, ten, eight, five, four, and three per cent. In Holland, it has even been as low as two per cent. Hence it is concluded, that "in proportion as society comes to perfection, it will descend to zero by the time civilization is complete. In other words, that which characterizes social perfection is the gratuitousness of credit. When, therefore, we shall have abolished interest, we shall have reached the last step of progress." This is mere sophistry, and as such false arguing may contribute to render popular the unjust, dangerous, and destructive dogma, that credit should be gratuitous, by representing it as coincident with social perfection, with the reader's permission I will examine in a few words this new view of the question.

What is *interest*? It is the service rendered, after a free bargain, by the borrower to the lender, in remuneration for the service he has received by the loan. By what law is the rate of these remunerative services established? By the general law which regulates the equivalent of all services; that is, by the law of supply and demand.

The more easily a thing is procured, the smaller is the service rendered by yielding it or lending it. The man who gives me a glass of water in the Pyrenees, does not render me so great a service as he who allows me one in the desert of Sahara. If there are many planes, sacks of corn, or houses, in a country, the use of them is obtained, other things being equal, on more favourable conditions than if they were few; for the simple reason, that the lender renders in this case a smaller *relative service*.

It is not surprising, therefore, that the more abundant capitals are, the lower is the interest.

Is this saying that it will ever reach zero? No; because, I repeat it, the principle of a remuneration is in the loan. To say that interest will be annihilated, is to say that there will never be any motive for saving, for denying ourselves, in order to form new capitals, nor even to preserve the old ones. In this case, the waste would immediately bring a void, and interest would directly reappear.

In that, the nature of the services of which we are speaking does not differ from any other. Thanks to industrial progress, a pair of stockings, which used to be worth six francs, has successively been worth only four, three, and two. No one can say to what point this value will descend; but we can affirm that it will never reach zero, unless the stockings finish by producing themselves spontaneously. Why? Because the principle of remuneration is in labour; because he who works for another renders a service, and ought to receive a service. If no one paid for stockings, they would cease to be made; and, with the scarcity, the price would not fail to reappear.

The sophism which I am now combating has its root in the infinite divisibility which belongs to *value*, as it does to matter.

It appears at first paradoxical, but it is well known to all mathematicians, that, through all eternity, fractions may be taken from a weight without the weight ever being annihilated. It is sufficient that each successive fraction be less than the preceding one, in a determined and regular proportion.

There are countries where people apply themselves to increasing the size of horses, or diminishing in sheep the size of the head. It is impossible to say precisely to what point they will arrive in this. No one can say that he has seen the largest horse or the smallest sheep's head that will ever appear in the world. But he may safely say that the size of horses will never attain to infinity, nor the heads of sheep to nothing.

In the same way, no one can say to what point the price of stockings nor the interest of capitals will come down; but we may safely affirm, when we know the nature of things, that neither the one nor the other will ever arrive at zero, for labour and capital can no more live without recompense than a sheep without a head.

The arguments of M. Proudhon reduce themselves, then, to this: Since the most skilful agriculturists are those who have reduced the heads of sheep to the smallest size, we shall have arrived at the highest agricultural perfection when sheep have no longer any heads. Therefore, in order to realize the perfection, let us behead them.

I have now done with this wearisome discussion. Why is it that the breath of false doctrine has made it needful to examine into the intimate nature of interest? I must not leave off without remarking upon a beautiful moral which may be drawn from this law: "The depression of interest is proportioned to the abundance of capitals." This law being granted, if there is a class of men to whom it is more important than to any other that capitals be formed, accumulate, multiply, abound, and superabound, it is certainly the class which borrows them directly or indirectly; it is those men who operate upon *materials*, who gain assistance by *instruments*, who live upon *provisions*, produced and economized by other men.

Imagine, in a vast and fertile country, a population of a thousand inhabitants, destitute of all capital thus defined. It will assuredly perish by the pangs of hunger. Let us suppose a case hardly less cruel. Let us suppose that ten of these savages are provided with instruments and provisions sufficient to work and to live themselves until harvest time, as well as to remunerate the services of eighty labourers. The inevitable result will be the death of nine hundred human beings. It is clear, then, that since nine hundred and ninety men, urged by want, will crowd upon the supports which would only maintain a hundred, the ten capitalists will be masters of the market. They will obtain labour on the hardest conditions, for they will put it up to auction, or the highest bidder. And observe this,—if these capitalists entertain such pious sentiments as would induce them to impose personal privations on themselves, in order to diminish the sufferings of some of their brethren, this generosity, which attaches to morality, will be as noble in its principle as useful in its effects. But if, duped by that false philosophy which persons wish so inconsiderately to mingle with economic laws, they take to remunerating labour largely, far from doing good, they will do harm. They will give double wages, it may be. But then, forty-five men will be better provided for, whilst forty-five others will come to augment the number of those who are sinking into the grave. Upon this supposition, it is not the lowering of wages which is the mischief, it is the scarcity of capital. Low wages are not the cause, but the effect of the evil. I may add, that they are to a certain extent the remedy. It acts in this way; it distributes the burden of suffering as much as it can, and saves as many lives as a limited quantity of sustenance permits.

Suppose now, that instead of ten capitalists, there should be a hundred, two hundred, five hundred,—is it not evident that the condition of the whole population, and, above all, that of the pro-létaires, will be more and more improved? Is it not evident that, apart from every consideration of generosity, they would obtain more work and better pay for it?—That they themselves will be in a better condition, to form capitals, without being able to fix the limits to this ever-increasing facility of realizing equality and well-being? Would it not be madness in them to admit such doctrines, and to act in a way which would drain the source of wages, and paralyze the activity and stimulus of saving? Let them learn this lesson, then; doubtless, capitals are good for those who possess them: Who denies it? But they are also useful to those who have not yet been able to form them; and it is important to those who have them not, that others should have them.

Yes, if the prolétaires knew their true interests, they would seek, with the greatest care, what circumstances are, and what are not favourable to saving, in order to favour the former and to discourage the latter. They would sympathize with every measure which tends to the rapid formation of capitals. They would be enthusiastic promoters of peace, liberty, order, security, the union of classes and peoples, econ-omy, moderation in public expenses, simplicity in the machinery of government; for it is under the sway of all these circumstances that saving does its work, brings plenty within the reach of the masses, invites those persons to become the formers of capital who were formerly under the necessity of borrowing upon hard conditions. They would repel with energy the warlike spirit, which diverts from its true course so large a part of human labour; the monopolizing spirit, which deranges the equitable distribution of riches, in the way by which liberty alone can realize it; the multitude of public services, which attack our purses only to check our liberty; and, in short, those subversive, hateful, thoughtless doctrines, which alarm capital, prevent its formation, oblige it to flee, and finally to raise its price, to the special disadvantage of the workers, who bring it into operation. Well, and in this respect is not the revolution of February a hard lesson? Is it not evident that the insecurity it has thrown into the world of business on the one hand; and, on the other, the advancement of the fatal theories to which I have alluded, and which, from the clubs, have almost penetrated into the regions of the legislature, have everywhere raised the rate of interest? Is it not evident, that from that time the prolétaires have found greater difficulty in procuring those materials, instruments, and provisions, without which labour is impossible? Is it not that which has caused stoppages; and do not stoppages, in their turn, lower wages? Thus, there is a deficiency of labour to the prolétaires, from the same cause which loads the objects they consume with an increase of price, in consequence of the rise of interest. High interest, low wages, means in other words that the same article preserves its price, but that the part of the capitalist has invaded, without profiting himself, that of the workmen.

A friend of mine, commissioned to make inquiry into Parisian industry, has assured me that the manufacturers have revealed to him a very striking fact, which proves, better than any reasoning can, how much insecurity and uncertainty injure the formation of capital. It was remarked, that during the most distressing period, the popular expenses of mere fancy had not diminished. The small theatres, the fighting lists, the public houses, and tobacco depots, were as much frequented as in prosperous times. In the inquiry, the operatives themselves explained this phenomenon thus: "What is the use of pinching? Who knows what will happen to us? Who knows that interest will not be abolished? Who knows but that the State will become a universal and gratuitous lender, and that it will wish to annihilate all the fruits which we might expect from our savings?" Well! I say, that if such ideas could prevail during two single years, it would be enough to turn our beautiful France into a Turkey—misery would become general and endemic, and, most assuredly, the poor would be the first upon whom it would fall.

Workmen! They talk to you a great deal upon the *artificial* organization of labour;—do you know why they do so? Because they are ignorant of the laws of its *natural* organization; that is, of the wonderful organization which results from liberty. You are told, that liberty gives rise to what is called the radical antagonism of classes; that it creates, and makes to clash, two opposite interests—that of the capitalists and that of the prolétaires. But we ought to begin by proving that this antagonism exists by a law of nature; and afterwards it would remain to be shown how far the arrangements of restraint are superior to those of liberty, for between liberty and restraint I see no middle path. Again, it would remain to be proved that restraint would always operate to your advantage, and to the prejudice of the rich. But, no; this radical antagonism, this natural opposition of interests, does not exist. It is only an evil dream of perverted and intoxicated imaginations. No; a plan so defective has not proceeded from the Divine Mind. To affirm it, we must begin by denying the existence of God. And see how, by means of social laws, and because men exchange amongst themselves their labours and their productions, see what a harmonious tie attaches the classes one to the other! There are the landowners; what is their interest? That the soil be fertile, and the sun beneficent; and what is the result? That corn abounds, that it falls in price, and the advantage turns to the profit of those who have had no patrimony. There are the manufacturers; what is their constant thought? To perfect their labour, to increase the power of their machines, to procure for themselves, upon the best terms, the raw material. And to what does all this tend? To the abundance and the low price of produce; that is, that all the efforts of the manufacturers, and without their suspecting it, result in a profit to the public consumer, of which each of you is one. It is the same with every profession. Well, the capitalists are not exempt from this law. They are very busy making schemes, economizing, and turning them to their advantage. This is all very well; but the more they succeed, the more do they promote the abundance of capital, and, as a necessary consequence, the reduction of interest. Now, who is it that profits by the reduction of interest? Is it not the borrower first, and finally, the consumers of the things which the capitals contribute to produce?

It is therefore certain that the final result of the efforts of each class is the common good of all.

You are told that capital tyrannizes over labour. I do not deny that each one endeavors to draw the greatest possible advantage from his situation; but, in this sense, he realizes only that which is possible. Now, it is never more possible for capitals to tyrannize over labour, than when they are scarce; for then it is they who make the law,—it is they who regulate the rate of sale. Never is this tyranny more impossible to them, than when they are abundant; for, in that case, it is labour which has the command.

Away, then, with the jealousies of classes, ill-will, unfounded hatreds, unjust suspicions. These depraved passions injure those who nourish them in their hearts. This is no declamatory morality; it is a chain of causes and effects, which is capable of being rigorously, mathematically demonstrated. It is not the less sublime, in that it satisfies the intellect as well as the feelings.

I shall sum up this whole dissertation with these words: Workmen, labourers, prolétaires, destitute and suffering classes, will you improve your condition? You will not succeed by strife, insurrection, hatred, and error. But there are three things which cannot perfect the entire community, without extending these benefits to yourselves; these things are: Peace, Liberty, and Security.

Notes

1. This error will be combated in a pamphlet, entitled *Cursed Money*.

Essays on Political Economy
Part II: That Which Is Seen, and That Which Is Not Seen

Frédéric Bastiat; 1848

In the department of economy, an act, a habit, an institution, a law, gives birth not only to an effect, but to a series of effects. Of these effects, the first only is immediate; it manifests itself simultaneously with its cause—it is seen. The others unfold in succession—they are not seen: It is well for us, if they are foreseen. Between a good and a bad economist this constitutes the whole difference—the one takes account of the visible effect; the other takes account both of the effects which are seen and also of those which it is necessary to foresee. Now this difference is enormous, for it almost always happens that when the immediate consequence is favourable, the ultimate consequences are fatal, and the converse. Hence it follows that the bad economist pursues a small present good, which will be followed by a great evil to come, while the true economist pursues a great good to come, at the risk of a small present evil.

In fact, it is the same in the science of health, arts, and in that of morals. It often happens, that the sweeter the first fruit of a habit is, the more bitter are the consequences. Take, for example, debauchery, idleness, prodigality. When, therefore, a man, absorbed in the effect which is seen, has not yet learned to discern those which are not seen, he gives way to fatal habits, not only by inclination, but by calculation.

This explains the fatally grievous condition of mankind. Ignorance surrounds its cradle; then its actions are determined by their first consequences, the only ones which, in its first stage, it can see. It is only in the long run that it learns to take account of the others. It has to learn this lesson from two very different masters—experience and foresight. Experience teaches effectually, but brutally. It makes us acquainted with all the effects of an action, by causing us to feel them; and we cannot fail to finish by knowing that fire burns, if we have burned ourselves. For this rough teacher, I should like, if possible, to substitute a more gentle

one. I mean Foresight. For this purpose I shall examine the consequences of certain economical phenomena, by placing in opposition to
each other those *which are seen*, and those *which are not seen*.

I. The Broken Window

Have you ever witnessed the anger of the good shopkeeper, James
B., when his careless son happened to break a pane of glass? If you have
been present at such a scene, you will most assuredly bear witness to
the fact, that every one of the spectators, were there even thirty of
them, by common consent apparently, offered the unfortunate owner
this invariable consolation: "It is an ill wind that blows nobody good.
Everybody must live, and what would become of the glaziers if panes of
glass were never broken?"

Now, this form of condolence contains an entire theory, which it
will be well to show up in this simple case, seeing that it is precisely the
same as that which, unhappily, regulates the greater part of our
economical institutions.

Suppose it cost six francs to repair the damage, and you say that
the accident brings six francs to the glazier's trade—that it encourages
that trade to the amount of six francs—I grant it; I have not a word to
say against it; you reason justly. The glazier comes, performs his task,
receives his six francs, rubs his hands, and, in his heart, blesses the
careless child. All this is that which is seen.

But if, on the other hand, you come to the conclusion, as is too
often the case, that it is a good thing to break windows, that it causes
money to circulate, and that the encouragement of industry in general
will be the result of it, you will oblige me to call out, "Stop there! Your
theory is confined to that which is seen; it takes no account of that
which is not seen."

It is not seen that as our shopkeeper has spent six francs upon one
thing, he cannot spend them upon another. It is not seen that if he had
not had a window to replace, he would, perhaps, have replaced his old
shoes, or added another book to his library. In short, he would have
employed his six francs in some way which this accident has prevented.

Let us take a view of industry in general, as affected by this
circumstance. The window being broken, the glazier's trade is encouraged to the amount of six francs; this is that which is seen. If the
window had not been broken, the shoemaker's trade (or some other)

would have been encouraged to the amount of six francs; this is that which is not seen.

And if that which is not seen is taken into consideration, because it is a negative fact, as well as that which is seen, because it is a positive fact, it will be understood that neither industry in general, nor the sum total of national labour, is affected, whether windows are broken or not.

Now let us consider James B. himself. In the former supposition, that of the window being broken, he spends six francs, and has neither more nor less than he had before, the enjoyment of a window.

In the second, where we suppose the window not to have been broken, he would have spent six francs on shoes, and would have had at the same time the enjoyment of a pair of shoes and of a window.

Now, as James B. forms a part of society, we must come to the conclusion, that, taking it altogether, and making an estimate of its enjoyments and its labours, it has lost the value of the broken window.

Whence we arrive at this unexpected conclusion: "Society loses the value of things which are uselessly destroyed;" and we must assent to a maxim which will make the hair of protectionists stand on end—To break, to spoil, to waste, is not to encourage national labour; or, more briefly, "destruction is not profit."

What will you say, *Moniteur Industriel*—what will you say, disciples of good M. F. Chamans, who has calculated with so much precision how much trade would gain by the burning of Paris, from the number of houses it would be necessary to rebuild?

I am sorry to disturb these ingenious calculations, as far as their spirit has been introduced into our legislation; but I beg him to begin them again, by taking into the account that which is not seen, and placing it alongside of that which is seen.

The reader must take care to remember that there are not two persons only, but three concerned in the little scene which I have submitted to his attention. One of them, James B., represents the consumer, reduced, by an act of destruction, to one enjoyment instead of two. Another, under the title of the glazier, shows us the producer, whose trade is encouraged by the accident. The third is the shoemaker (or some other tradesman), whose labour suffers proportionably by the same cause. It is this third person who is always kept in the shade, and who, personating that which is not seen, is a necessary element of the problem. It is he who shows us how absurd it is to think we see a profit in an act of destruction. It is he who will soon teach us that it is not less absurd to see a profit in a restriction, which is, after all, nothing else than a partial destruction. Therefore, if you will only go to the root of all the arguments which are adduced in its favour, all you will find will be the paraphrase of this vulgar saying: What would become of the glaziers, if nobody ever broke windows?

II. The Disbanding of Troops

It is the same with a people as it is with a man. If it wishes to give itself some gratification, it naturally considers whether it is worth what it costs. To a nation, security is the greatest of advantages. If, in order to obtain it, it is necessary to have an army of a hundred thousand men, I have nothing to say against it. It is an enjoyment bought by a sacrifice. Let me not be misunderstood upon the extent of my position. A member of the assembly proposes to disband a hundred thousand men, for the sake of relieving the tax-payers of a hundred millions.

If we confine ourselves to this answer: "The hundred millions of men, and these hundred millions of money, are indispensable to the national security: It is a sacrifice; but without this sacrifice, France would be torn by factions or invaded by some foreign power,"—I have nothing to object to this argument, which may be true or false in fact, but which theoretically contains nothing which militates against economy. The error begins when the sacrifice itself is said to be an advantage because it profits somebody.

Now I am very much mistaken if, the moment the author of the proposal has taken his seat, some orator will not rise and say, "Disband a hundred thousand men! Do you know what you are saying? What will become of them? Where will they get a living? Don't you know that work is scarce everywhere? That every field is overstocked? Would you turn them out of doors to increase competition and to weigh upon the rate of wages? Just now, when it is a hard matter to live at all, it would be a pretty thing if the State must find bread for a hundred thousand individuals? Consider, besides, that the army consumes wine, arms, clothing—that it promotes the activity of manufactures in garrison towns—that it is, in short, the godsend of innumerable purveyors. Why, any one must tremble at the bare idea of doing away with this immense industrial movement."

This discourse, it is evident, concludes by voting the maintenance of a hundred thousand soldiers, for reasons drawn from the necessity of the service, and from economical considerations. It is these considerations only that I have to refute.

A hundred thousand men, costing the tax-payers a hundred millions of money, live and bring to the purveyors as much as a hundred millions can supply. This is that which is seen.

But, a hundred millions taken from the pockets of the tax-payers, cease to maintain these tax-payers and the purveyors, as far as a hundred millions reach. This is *that which is not seen*. Now make your calculations. Cast up, and tell me what profit there is for the masses?

I will tell you where the loss lies; and to simplify it, instead of speaking of a hundred thousand men and a million of money, it shall be of one man and a thousand francs.

We will suppose that we are in the village of A. The recruiting sergeants go their round, and take off a man. The tax-gatherers go their round, and take off a thousand francs. The man and the sum of money are taken to Metz, and the latter is destined to support the former for a year without doing anything. If you consider Metz only, you are quite right; the measure is a very advantageous one: But if you look towards the village of A., you will judge very differently; for, unless you are very blind indeed, you will see that that village has lost a worker, and the thousand francs which would remunerate his labour, as well as the activity which, by the expenditure of those thousand francs, it would spread around it.

At first sight, there would seem to be some compensation. What took place at the village, now takes place at Metz, that is all. But the loss is to be estimated in this way: At the village, a man dug and worked; he was a worker. At Metz, he turns to the right about and to the left about; he is a soldier. The money and the circulation are the same in both cases; but in the one there were three hundred days of productive labour, in the other there are three hundred days of unproductive labour, supposing, of course, that a part of the army is not indispensable to the public safety.

Now, suppose the disbanding to take place. You tell me there will be a surplus of a hundred thousand workers, that competition will be stimulated, and it will reduce the rate of wages. This is what you see.

But what you do not see is this. You do not see that to dismiss a hundred thousand soldiers is not to do away with a million of money, but to return it to the tax-payers. You do not see that to throw a hundred thousand workers on the market, is to throw into it, at the same moment, the hundred millions of money needed to pay for their labour;

that, consequently, the same act which increases the supply of hands, increases also the demand; from which it follows, that your fear of a reduction of wages is unfounded. You do not see that, before the disbanding as well as after it, there are in the country a hundred millions of money corresponding with the hundred thousand men. That the whole difference consists in this: Before the disbanding, the country gave the hundred millions to the hundred thousand men for doing nothing; and that after it, it pays them the same sum for working. You do not see, in short, that when a tax-payer gives his money either to a soldier in exchange for nothing, or to a worker in exchange for something, all the ultimate consequences of the circulation of this money are the same in the two cases; only, in the second case the tax-payer receives something, in the former he receives nothing. The result is—a dead loss to the nation.

The sophism which I am here combating will not stand the test of progression, which is the touchstone of principles. If, when every compensation is made, and all interests satisfied, there is a national profit in increasing the army, why not enroll under its banners the entire male population of the country?

III. Taxes

Have you ever chanced to hear it said, "There is no better investment than taxes. Only see what a number of families it maintains, and consider how it reacts upon industry; it is an inexhaustible stream, it is life itself."

In order to combat this doctrine, I must refer to my preceding refutation. Political economy knew well enough that its arguments were not so amusing that it could be said of them, *repetitions please*. It has, therefore, turned the proverb to its own use, well convinced that, in its mouth, *repetitions teach*.

The advantages which officials advocate are those which are seen. The benefit which accrues to the providers is still that which is seen. This blinds all eyes.

But the disadvantages which the tax-payers have to get rid of are those which are not seen. And the injury which results from it to the providers is still that which is not seen, although this ought to be self-evident.

When an official spends for his own profit an extra hundred sous, it implies that a tax-payer spends for his profit a hundred sous less. But the expense of the official is seen, because the act is performed, while that of the tax-payer is not seen, because, alas! he is prevented from performing it.

You compare the nation, perhaps to a parched tract of land, and the tax to a fertilizing rain. Be it so. But you ought also to ask yourself where are the sources of this rain, and whether it is not the tax itself which draws away the moisture from the ground and dries it up?

Again, you ought to ask yourself whether it is possible that the soil can receive as much of this precious water by rain as it loses by evaporation?

There is one thing very certain, that when James B. counts out a hundred sous for the tax-gatherer, he receives nothing in return. Afterwards, when an official spends these hundred sous, and returns them to James B., it is for an equal value in corn or labour. The final result is a loss to James B. of five francs.

It is very true that often, perhaps very often, the official performs for James B. an equivalent service. In this case there is no loss on either side; there is merely an exchange. Therefore, my arguments do not at all apply to useful functionaries. All I say is,—if you wish to create an office, prove its utility. Show that its value to James B., by the services which it performs for him, is equal to what it costs him. But, apart from this intrinsic utility, do not bring forward as an argument the benefit which it confers upon the official, his family, and his providers; do not assert that it encourages labour.

When James B. gives a hundred sous to a government officer for a really useful service, it is exactly the same as when he gives a hundred sous to a shoemaker for a pair of shoes.

But when James B. gives a hundred sous to a government officer, and receives nothing for them unless it be annoyances, he might as well give them to a thief. It is nonsense to say that the government officer will spend these hundred sous to the great profit of national labour; the thief would do the same; and so would James B., if he had not been stopped on the road by the extra-legal parasite, nor by the lawful sponger.

Let us accustom ourselves, then, to avoid judging of things by what is seen only, but to judge of them by that which is not seen.

Last year I was on the Committee of Finance, for under the constituency the members of the opposition were not systematically excluded from all the Commissions; in that the constituency acted wisely. We have heard M. Thiers say: "I have passed my life in opposing the legitimist party, and the priest party. Since the common danger has brought us together, now that I associate with them and know them, and now that we speak face to face, I have found out that they are not the monsters I used to imagine them."

Yes, distrust is exaggerated, hatred is fostered among parties who never mix; and if the majority would allow the minority to be present at the Commissions, it would perhaps be discovered that the ideas of the different sides are not so far removed from each other; and, above all, that their intentions are not so perverse as is supposed. However, last year I was on the Committee of Finance. Every time that one of our colleagues spoke of fixing at a moderate figure the maintenance of the President of the Republic, that of the ministers, and of the ambassadors, it was answered:

"For the good of the service, it is necessary to surround certain offices with splendour and dignity, as a means of attracting men of merit to them. A vast number of unfortunate persons apply to the President of the Republic, and it would be placing him in a very painful position to oblige him to be constantly refusing them. A certain style in the ministerial saloons is a part of the machinery of constitutional governments."

Although such arguments may be controverted, they certainly deserve a serious examination. They are based upon the public interest, whether rightly estimated or not; and as far as I am concerned, I have much more respect for them than many of our Catos have, who are actuated by a narrow spirit of parsimony or of jealousy.

But what revolts the economical part of my conscience, and makes me blush for the intellectual resources of my country, is when this absurd relic of feudalism is brought forward, which it constantly is, and it is favourably received too:

"Besides, the luxury of great government officers encourages the arts, industry, and labour. The head of the State and his ministers cannot give banquets and soirées without causing life to circulate through all the veins of the social

body. To reduce their means, would starve Parisian industry, and consequently that of the whole nation."

I must beg you, gentlemen, to pay some little regard to arithmetic,
at least; and not to say before the National Assembly in France, lest to
its shame it should agree with you, that an addition gives a different
sum, according to whether it is added up from the bottom to the top, or
from the top to the bottom of the column.

For instance, I want to agree with a drainer to make a trench in my
field for a hundred sous. Just as we have concluded our arrangement
the tax-gatherer comes, takes my hundred sous, and sends them to the
Minister of the Interior; my bargain is at end, but the minister will have
another dish added to his table. Upon what ground will you dare to
affirm that this official expense helps the national industry? Do you not
see, that in this there is only a reversing of satisfaction and labour? A
minister has his table better covered, it is true; but it is just as true that
an agriculturist has his field worse drained. A Parisian tavern-keeper has
gained a hundred sous, I grant you; but then you must grant me that a
drainer has been prevented from gaining five francs. It all comes to
this,—that the official and the tavern-keeper being satisfied, is that
which is seen; the field undrained, and the drainer deprived of his job, is
that which is not seen. Dear me! How much trouble there is in proving
that two and two make four; and if you succeed in proving it, it is said
"the thing is so plain it is quite tiresome," and they vote as if you had
proved nothing at all.

IV. Theatres and Fine Arts

Ought the State to support the arts?

There is certainly much to be said on both sides of this question. It
may be said, in favour of the system of voting supplies for this purpose,
that the arts enlarge, elevate, and harmonize the soul of a nation; that
they divert it from too great an absorption in material occupations;
encourage in it a love for the beautiful; and thus act favourably on its
manners, customs, morals, and even on its industry. It may be asked,
what would become of music in France without her Italian theatre and
her Conservatoire; of the dramatic art, without her Théâtre-Français; of
painting and sculpture, without our collections, galleries, and museums?

It might even be asked, whether, without centralization, and consequently the support of the fine arts, that exquisite taste would be developed which is the noble appendage of French labour, and which introduces its productions to the whole world? In the face of such results, would it not be the height of imprudence to renounce this moderate contribution from all her citizens, which, in fact, in the eyes of Europe, realizes their superiority and their glory?

To these and many other reasons, whose force I do not dispute, arguments no less forcible may be opposed. It might first of all be said, that there is a question of distributive justice in it. Does the right of the legislator extend to abridging the wages of the artisan, for the sake of, adding to the profits of the artist? M. Lamartine said, "If you cease to support the theatre, where will you stop? Will you not necessarily be led to withdraw your support from your colleges, your museums, your institutes, and your libraries? It might be answered, if you desire to support everything which is good and useful, where will you stop? Will you not necessarily be led to form a civil list for agriculture, industry, commerce, benevolence, education? Then, is it certain that government aid favours the progress of art?

This question is far from being settled, and we see very well that the theatres which prosper are those which depend upon their own resources. Moreover, if we come to higher considerations, we may observe that wants and desires arise the one from the other, and originate in regions which are more and more refined in proportion as the public wealth allows of their being satisfied; that government ought not to take part in this correspondence, because in a certain condition of present fortune it could not by taxation stimulate the arts of necessity without checking those of luxury, and thus interrupting the natural course of civilization. I may observe, that these artificial transpositions of wants, tastes, labour, and population, place the people in a precarious and dangerous position, without any solid basis."

These are some of the reasons alleged by the adversaries of State intervention in what concerns the order in which citizens think their wants and desires should be satisfied, and to which, consequently, their activity should be directed. I am, I confess, one of those who think that choice and impulse ought to come from below and not from above, from the citizen and not from the legislator; and the opposite doctrine appears to me to tend to the destruction of liberty and of human dignity.

But, by a deduction as false as it is unjust, do you know what economists are accused of? It is, that when we disapprove of government support, we are supposed to disapprove of the thing itself whose support is discussed; and to be the enemies of every kind of activity, because we desire to see those activities, on the one hand free, and on the other seeking their own reward in themselves. Thus, if we think that the State should not interfere by taxation in religious affairs, we are atheists. If we think the State ought not to interfere by taxation in education, we are hostile to knowledge. If we say that the State ought not by taxation to give a fictitious value to land, or to any particular branch of industry, we are enemies to property and labour. If we think that the State ought not to support artists, we are barbarians, who look upon the arts as useless.

Against such conclusions as these I protest with all my strength. Far from entertaining the absurd idea of doing away with religion, education, property, labour, and the arts, when we say that the State ought to protect the free development of all these kinds of human activity, without helping some of them at the expense of others—we think, on the contrary, that all these living powers of society would develop themselves more harmoniously under the influence of liberty; and that, under such an influence no one of them would, as is now the case, be a source of trouble, of abuses, of tyranny, and disorder.

Our adversaries consider that an activity which is neither aided by supplies, nor regulated by government, is an activity destroyed. We think just the contrary. Their faith is in the legislator, not in mankind; ours is in mankind, not in the legislator.

Thus, M. Lamartine said, "Upon this principle we must abolish the public exhibitions, which are the honour and the wealth of this country." But I would say to M. Lamartine,—According to your way of thinking, not to support is to abolish; because, setting out upon the maxim that nothing exists independently of the will of the State, you conclude that nothing lives but what the State causes to live. But I oppose to this assertion the very example which you have chosen, and beg you to remark, that the grandest and noblest of exhibitions, one which has been conceived in the most liberal and universal spirit—and I might even make use of the term humanitary, for it is no exaggeration—is the exhibition now preparing in London; the only one in which no government is taking any part, and which is being paid for by no tax.

To return to the fine arts: There are, I repeat, many strong reasons to be brought, both for and against the system of government assistance. The reader must see that the especial object of this work leads me neither to explain these reasons, nor to decide in their favour, nor against them.

But M. Lamartine has advanced one argument which I cannot pass by in silence, for it is closely connected with this economic study. "The economical question, as regards theatres, is comprised in one word—labour. It matters little what is the nature of this labour; it is as fertile, as productive a labour as any other kind of labour in the nation. The theatres in France, you know, feed and salary no less than eighty thousand workmen of different kinds; painters, masons, decorators, costumers, architects, etc., which constitute the very life and movement of several parts of this capital, and on this account they ought to have your sympathies." Your sympathies! Say, rather, your money.

And further on he says: "The pleasures of Paris are the labour and the consumption of the provinces, and the luxuries of the rich are the wages and bread of two hundred thousand workmen of every description, who live by the manifold industry of the theatres on the surface of the republic, and who receive from these noble pleasures, which render France illustrious, the sustenance of their lives and the necessaries of their families and children. It is to them that you will give sixty thousand francs." (Very well; very well. Great applause.) For my part I am constrained to say, "Very bad! Very bad!" Confining this opinion, of course, within the bounds of the economical question which we are discussing.

Yes, it is to the workmen of the theatres that a part, at least, of these sixty thousand francs will go; a few bribes, perhaps, may be abstracted on the way. Perhaps, if we were to look a little more closely into the matter, we might find that the cake had gone another way, and that those workmen were fortunate who had come in for a few crumbs. But I will allow, for the sake of argument, that the entire sum does go to the painters, decorators, etc.

This is that which is seen. But whence does it come? This is the other side of the question, and quite as important as the former. Where do these sixty thousand francs spring from? And where would they go, if a vote of the legislature did not direct them first towards the Rue Rivoli and thence towards the Rue Grenelle? This is what is not seen. Certainly, nobody will think of maintaining that the legislative vote has caused this sum to be hatched in a ballot urn; that it is a pure addition made to the national wealth; that but for this miraculous vote these sixty thousand francs would have been for ever invisible and impalpable. It must be admitted that all that the majority can do is to decide that they shall be taken from one place to be sent to another; and if they take one direction, it is only because they have been diverted from another.

This being the case, it is clear that the tax-payer, who has contributed one franc, will no longer have this franc at his own disposal. It is clear that he will be deprived of some gratification to the amount of one franc; and that the workman, whoever he may be, who would have received it from him, will be deprived of a benefit to that amount. Let us not, therefore, be led by a childish illusion into believing that the vote of the sixty thousand francs may add anything whatever to the well-being of the country, and to national labour. It displaces enjoyments, it transposes wages—that is all.

Will it be said that for one kind of gratification, and one kind of labour, it substitutes more urgent, more moral, more reasonable gratifications and labour? I might dispute this; I might say, by taking sixty thousand francs from the tax-payers, you diminish the wages of labourers, drainers, carpenters, blacksmiths, and increase in proportion those of the singers.

There is nothing to prove that this latter class calls for more sympathy than the former. M. Lamartine does not say that it is so. He himself says that the labour of the theatres is as fertile, as productive as any other (not more so); and this may be doubted; for the best proof that the latter is not so fertile as the former lies in this, that the other is to be called upon to assist it.

But this comparison between the value and the intrinsic merit of different kinds of labour forms no part of my present subject. All I have to do here is to show, that if M. Lamartine and those persons who commend his line of argument have seen on one side the salaries gained by the providers of the comedians, they ought on the other to have seen the salaries lost by the providers of the tax-payers; for want of this, they have exposed themselves to ridicule by mistaking a displacement for a gain. If they were true to their doctrine, there would be no limits to their demands for government aid; for that which is true of one franc and of sixty thousand is true, under parallel circumstances, of a hundred millions of francs.

When taxes are the subject of discussion, you ought to prove their utility by reasons from the root of the matter, but not by this unlucky assertion: "The public expenses support the working classes." This assertion disguises the important fact, that public expenses always supersede private expenses, and that therefore we bring a livelihood to one workman instead of another, but add nothing to the share of the working class as a whole. Your arguments are fashionable enough, but they are too absurd to be justified by anything like reason.

V. Public Works

Nothing is more natural than that a nation, after having assured itself that an enterprise will benefit the community, should have it executed by means of a general assessment. But I lose patience, I confess, when I hear this economic blunder advanced in support of such a project: "Besides, it will be a means of creating labour for the workmen."

The State opens a road, builds a palace, straightens a street, cuts a canal, and so gives work to certain workmen—this is what is seen: But it deprives certain other workmen of work, and this is what is not seen.

The road is begun. A thousand workmen come every morning, leave every evening, and take their wages—this is certain. If the road had not been decreed, if the supplies had not been voted, these good people would have had neither work nor salary there; this also is certain.

But is this all? Does not the operation, as a whole, contain something else? At the moment when M. Dupin pronounces the emphatic words, "The Assembly has adopted," do the millions descend miraculously on a moonbeam into the coffers of MM. Fould and Bineau? In order that the evolution may be complete, as it is said, must not the State organize the receipts as well as the expenditure? Must it not set its tax-gatherers and tax-payers to work, the former to gather and the latter to pay?

Study the question, now, in both its elements. While you state the destination given by the State to the millions voted, do not neglect to state also the destination which the tax-payer would have given, but cannot now give, to the same. Then you will understand that a public enterprise is a coin with two sides. Upon one is engraved a labourer at work, with this device, that which is seen; on the other is a labourer out of work, with the device, that which is not seen.

The sophism which this work is intended to refute is the more dangerous when applied to public works, inasmuch as it serves to justify the most wanton enterprises and extravagance. When a railroad or a bridge are of real utility, it is sufficient to mention this utility. But if it does not exist, what do they do? Recourse is had to this mystification: "We must find work for the workmen."

Accordingly, orders are given that the drains in the Champ-de-Mars be made and unmade. The great Napoleon, it is said, thought he was doing a very philanthropic work by causing ditches to be made and then filled up. He said, therefore, "What signifies the result? All we want is to see wealth spread among the labouring classes."

But let us go to the root of the matter. We are deceived by money. To demand the cooperation of all the citizens in a common work, in the form of money, is in reality to demand a concurrence in kind; for every one procures, by his own labour, the sum to which he is taxed. Now, if all the citizens were to be called together, and made to execute, in conjunction, a work useful to all, this would be easily understood; their reward would be found in the results of the work itself.

But after having called them together, if you force them to make roads which no one will pass through, palaces which no one will inhabit, and this under the pretext of finding them work, it would be absurd, and they would have a right to argue, "With this labour we have nothing to do; we prefer working on our own account."

A proceeding which consists in making the citizens cooperate in giving money but not labour, does not, in any way, alter the general results. The only thing is, that the loss would react upon all parties. By the former, those whom the State employs, escape their part of the loss, by adding it to that which their fellow-citizens have already suffered.

There is an article in our constitution which says: "Society favours and encourages the development of labour—by the establishment of public works, by the State, the departments, and the parishes, as a means of employing persons who are in want of work."

As a temporary measure, on any emergency, during a hard winter, this interference with the tax-payers may have its use. It acts in the same way as securities. It adds nothing either to labour or to wages, but it takes labour and wages from ordinary times to give them, at a loss it is true, to times of difficulty.

As a permanent, general, systematic measure, it is nothing else than a ruinous mystification, an impossibility, which shows a little excited labour which is seen, and hides a great deal of prevented labour which is not seen.

VI. The Intermediates

Society is the total of the forced or voluntary services which men perform for each other; that is to say, of public services and private services.

The former, imposed and regulated by the law, which it is not always easy to change, even when it is desirable, may survive with it their own usefulness, and still preserve the name of public services, even when they are no longer services at all, but rather public annoyances. The latter belong to the sphere of the will, of individual responsibility. Every one gives and receives what he wishes, and what he can, after a debate. They have always the presumption of real utility, in exact proportion to their comparative value.

This is the reason why the former description of services so often become stationary, while the latter obey the law of progress.

While the exaggerated development of public services, by the waste of strength which it involves, fastens upon society a fatal sycophancy, it is a singular thing that several modern sects, attributing this character to free and private services, are endeavoring to transform professions into functions.

These sects violently oppose what they call intermediates. They would gladly suppress the capitalist, the banker, the speculator, the projector, the merchant, and the trader, accusing them of interposing between production and consumption, to extort from both, without giving either anything in return. Or rather, they would transfer to the State the work which they accomplish, for this work cannot be suppressed.

The sophism of the Socialists on this point is showing to the public what it pays to the intermediates in exchange for their services, and concealing from it what is necessary to be paid to the State. Here is the usual conflict between what is before our eyes and what is perceptible to the mind only; between what is seen and what is not seen.

It was at the time of the scarcity, in 1847, that the Socialist schools attempted and succeeded in popularizing their fatal theory. They knew very well that the most absurd notions have always a chance with people who are suffering; *malisuada fames*.

Therefore, by the help of the fine words, "trafficking in men by men, speculation on hunger, monopoly," they began to blacken commerce, and to cast a veil over its benefits.

"What can be the use," they say, "of leaving to the merchants the care of importing food from the United States and the Crimea? Why do not the State, the departments, and the towns, organize a service for provisions and a magazine for stores? They would sell at a return price, and the people, poor things, would be exempted from the tribute which they pay to free, that is, to egotistical, individual, and anarchical commerce."

The tribute paid by the people to commerce is that which is seen. The tribute which the people would pay to the State, or to its agents, in the Socialist system, is what is not seen.

In what does this pretended tribute, which the people pay to commerce, consist? In this: That two men render each other a mutual service, in all freedom, and under the pressure of competition and reduced prices.

When the hungry stomach is at Paris, and corn which can satisfy it is at Odessa, the suffering cannot cease till the corn is brought into contact with the stomach. There are three means by which this contact may be effected. 1st. The famished men may go themselves and fetch the corn. 2nd. They may leave this task to those to whose trade it belongs. 3rd. They may club together, and give the office in charge to public functionaries. Which of these three methods possesses the greatest advantages? In every time, in all countries, and the more free, enlightened, and experienced they are, men have *voluntarily* chosen the second. I confess that this is sufficient, in my opinion, to justify this choice. I cannot believe that mankind, as a whole, is deceiving itself upon a point which touches it so nearly. But let us now consider the subject.

For thirty-six millions of citizens to go and fetch the corn they want from Odessa, is a manifest impossibility. The first means, then, goes for nothing. The consumers cannot act for themselves. They must, of necessity, have recourse to intermediates, officials or agents.

But observe, that the first of these three means would be the most natural. In reality, the hungry man has to fetch his corn. It is a task which concerns himself, a service due to himself. If another person, on whatever ground, performs this service for him, takes the task upon himself, this latter has a claim upon him for a compensation. I mean by this to say that intermediates contain in themselves the principle of remuneration.

However that may be, since we must refer to what the Socialists call a parasite, I would ask, which of the two is the most exacting parasite, the merchant or the official?

Commerce (free, of course, otherwise I could not reason upon it), commerce, I say, is led by its own interests to study the seasons, to give daily statements of the state of the crops, to receive information from every part of the globe, to foresee wants, to take precautions beforehand. It has vessels always ready, correspondents everywhere; and it is its immediate interest to buy at the lowest possible price, to economize in all the details of its operations, and to attain the greatest results by the smallest efforts. It is not the French merchants only who are occupied in procuring provisions for France in time of need, and if their interest leads them irresistibly to accomplish their task at the smallest possible cost, the competition which they create amongst each other leads them no less irresistibly to cause the consumers to partake of the profits of those realized savings. The corn arrives; it is to the interest of commerce to sell it as soon as possible, so as to avoid risks, to realize its funds, and begin again the first opportunity.

Directed by the comparison of prices, it distributes food over the whole surface of the country, beginning always at the highest price, that is, where the demand is the greatest. It is impossible to imagine an organization more completely calculated to meet the interest of those who are in want; and the beauty of this organization, unperceived as it is by the Socialists, results from the very fact that it is free. It is true, the consumer is obliged to reimburse commerce for the expenses of conveyance, freight, store-room, commission, etc.; but can any system be devised in which he who eats corn is not obliged to defray the expenses, whatever they may be, of bringing it within his reach? The remuneration for the service performed has to be paid also; but as regards its amount, this is reduced to the smallest possible sum by competition; and as regards its justice, it would be very strange if the artisans of Paris would not work for the merchants of Marseilles, when the merchants of Marseilles work for the artisans of Paris.

If, according to the Socialist invention, the State were to stand in the stead of commerce, what would happen? I should like to be informed where the saving would be to the public? Would it be in the price of purchase? Imagine the delegates of forty thousand parishes arriving at Odessa on a given day, and on the day of need; imagine the effect upon prices. Would the saving be in the expenses? Would fewer vessels be required; fewer sailors, fewer transports, fewer sloops, or would you be exempt from the payment of all these things? Would it be in the profits of the merchants? Would your officials go to Odessa for nothing? Would they travel and work on the principle of fraternity? Must they not live? Must not they be paid for their time? And do you believe that these expenses would not exceed a thousand times the two or three per cent which the merchant gains, at the rate at which he is ready to treat?

And then consider the difficulty of levying so many taxes, and of dividing so much food. Think of the injustice, of the abuses inseparable from such an enterprise. Think of the responsibility which would weigh upon the government.

The Socialists who have invented these follies, and who, in the days of distress, have introduced them into the minds of the masses, take to themselves literally the title of advanced men; and it is not without some danger that custom, that tyrant of tongues, authorizes the term, and the sentiment which it involves. Advanced! This supposes that these gentlemen can see further than the common people; that their only fault is that they are too much in advance of their age; and if the time is not yet come for suppressing certain free services, pretended parasites, the fault is to be attributed to the public which is in the rear of Socialism. I say, from my soul and my conscience, the reverse is the truth; and I know not to what barbarous age we should have to go back, if we would find the level of Socialist knowledge on this subject. These modern sectarians incessantly oppose association to actual society. They overlook the fact that society, under a free regulation, is a true association, far superior to any of those which proceed from their fertile imaginations.

Let me illustrate this by an example. Before a man, when he gets up in the morning, can put on a coat, ground must have been enclosed, broken up, drained, tilled, and sown with a particular kind of plant; flocks must have been fed, and have given their wool; this wool must have been spun, woven, dyed, and converted into cloth; this cloth must have been cut, sewed, and made into a garment. And this series of operations implies a number of others; it supposes the employment of instruments for ploughing, sheepfolds, sheds, coal, machines, carriages, etc.

If society were not a perfectly real association, a person who wanted a coat would be reduced to the necessity of working in solitude; that is, of performing for himself the innumerable parts of this series, from the first stroke of the pickaxe to the last stitch which concludes the work. But, thanks to the sociability which is the distinguishing character of our race, these operations are distributed amongst a multitude of workers; and they are further subdivided, for the common good, to an extent that, as the consumption becomes more active, one single operation is able to support a new trade.

Then comes the division of the profits, which operates according to the contingent value which each has brought to the entire work. If this is not association, I should like to know what is.

Observe, that as no one of these workers has obtained the smallest particle of matter from nothingness, they are confined to performing for each other mutual services, and to helping each other in a common object, and that all may be considered, with respect to others, intermediates. If, for instance, in the course of the operation, the conveyance becomes important enough to occupy one person, the spinning another, the weaving another, why should the first be considered a parasite more than the other two? The conveyance must be made, must it not? Does not he who performs it, devote to it his time and trouble? And by so doing does he not spare that of his colleagues? Do these do more or other than this for him? Are they not equally dependent for remuneration, that is, for the division of the produce, upon the law of reduced price? Is it not in all liberty, for the common good, that these arrangements are entered into? What do we want with a Socialist then, who, under pretense of organizing for us, comes despotically to break up our voluntary arrangements, to check the division of labour, to substitute isolated efforts for combined ones, and to send civilization back? Is association, as I describe it here, in itself less association, because every one enters and leaves it freely, chooses his place in it, judges and bargains for himself on his own responsibility, and brings with him the spring and warrant of personal interest? That it may deserve this name, is it necessary that a pretended reformer should come and impose upon us his plan and his will, and as it were, to concentrate mankind in himself?

The more we examine these advanced schools, the more do we become convinced that there is but one thing at the root of them: Ignorance proclaiming itself infallible, and claiming despotism in the name of this infallibility.

I hope the reader will excuse this digression. It may not be altogether useless, at a time when declamations, springing from St. Simonian, Phalansterian, and Icarian books, are invoking the press and the tribune, and which seriously threaten the liberty of labour and commercial transactions.

VII. Restrictions

M. Prohibant (it was not I who gave him this name, but M. Charles Dupin) devoted his time and capital to converting the ore found on his land into iron. As nature had been more lavish towards the Belgians, they furnished the French with iron cheaper than M. Prohibant; which means, that all the French, or France, could obtain a given quantity of iron with less labour by buying it of the honest Flemings. Therefore, guided by their own interest, they did not fail to do so; and every day there might be seen a multitude of nail-smiths, blacksmiths, cartwrights, machinists, farriers, and labourers, going themselves, or sending intermediates, to supply themselves in Belgium. This displeased M. Prohibant exceedingly.

At first, it occurred to him to put an end to this abuse by his own efforts; it was the least he could do, for he was the only sufferer. "I will take my carbine," said he; "I will put four pistols into my belt; I will fill my cartridge box; I will gird on my sword, and go thus equipped to the frontier. There, the first blacksmith, nail-smith, farrier, machinist, or locksmith, who presents himself to do his own business and not mine, I will kill, to teach him how to live." At the moment of starting, M. Prohibant made a few reflections which calmed down his warlike ardour a little. He said to himself, "In the first place, it is not absolutely impossible that the purchasers of iron, my countrymen and enemies, should take the thing ill, and, instead of letting me kill them, should kill me instead; and then, even were I to call out all my servants, we should not be able to defend the passages. In short, this proceeding would cost me very dear, much more so than the result would be worth."

M. Prohibant was on the point of resigning himself to his sad fate, that of being only as free as the rest of the world, when a ray of light darted across his brain. He recollected that at Paris there is a great manufactory of laws. "What is a law?" said he to himself. "It is a measure to which, when once it is decreed, be it good or bad, everybody is bound to conform. For the execution of the same a public force is organized, and to constitute the said public force, men and money are drawn from the whole nation. If, then, I could only get the great Parisian manufactory to pass a little law, 'Belgian iron is prohibited,' I should obtain the following results: The government would replace the few valets that I was going to send to the frontier by twenty thousand of the sons of those refractory blacksmiths, farriers, artisans, machinists, locksmiths, nail-smiths, and labourers. Then to keep these twenty thousand custom-house officers in health and good humour, it would distribute among them twenty five-five millions of francs taken from these blacksmiths, nail-smiths, artisans, and labourers. They would guard the frontier much better; would cost me nothing; I should not be exposed to the brutality of the brokers, should sell the iron at my own price, and have the sweet satisfaction of seeing our great people shamefully mystified. That would teach them to proclaim themselves perpetually the harbingers and promoters of progress in Europe. Oh! It would be a capital joke, and deserves to be tried."

So M. Prohibant went to the law manufactory. Another time, perhaps, I shall relate the story of his underhand dealings, but now I shall merely mention his visible proceedings. He brought the following consideration before the view of the legislating gentlemen.

"Belgian iron is sold in France at ten francs, which obliges me to sell mine at the same price. I should like to sell at fifteen, but cannot do so on account of this Belgian iron, which I wish was at the bottom of the Red Sea. I beg you will make a law that no more Belgian iron shall enter France. Immediately I raise my price five francs, and these are the consequences:

"For every hundred-weight of iron that I shall deliver to the public, I shall receive fifteen francs instead of ten; I shall grow rich more rapidly, extend my traffic, and employ more workmen. My workmen and I shall spend much more freely, to the great advantage of our tradesmen for miles around. These latter, having more custom, will furnish more employment to trade, and activity on both sides will increase in the country. This fortunate piece of money, which you will drop into my strong-box, will, like a stone thrown into a lake, give birth to an infinite number of concentric circles."

Charmed with his discourse, delighted to learn that it is so easy to promote, by legislating, the prosperity of a people, the law-makers voted the restriction. "Talk of labour and economy," they said, "what is the use of these painful means of increasing the national wealth, when all that is wanted for this object is a decree?"

And, in fact, the law produced all the consequences announced by M. Prohibant; the only thing was, it produced others which he had not foreseen. To do him justice, his reasoning was not false, but only incomplete. In endeavoring to obtain a privilege, he had taken cognizance of the effects which are seen, leaving in the background those which are not seen. He had pointed out only two personages, whereas there are three concerned in the affair. It is for us to supply this involuntary or premeditated omission.

It is true, the crown-piece, thus directed by law into M. Prohibant's strong-box, is advantageous to him and to those whose labour it would encourage; and if the Act had caused the crown-piece to descend from the moon, these good effects would not have been counterbalanced by any corresponding evils. Unfortunately, the mysterious piece of money does not come from the moon, but from the pocket of a blacksmith, or a nail-smith, or a cartwright, or a farrier, or a labourer, or a shipwright; in a word, from James B., who gives it now without receiving a grain more of iron than when he was paying ten francs. Thus, we can see at a glance that this very much alters the state of the case; for it is very evident that M. Prohibant's profit is compensated by James B.'s loss, and all that M. Prohibant can do with the crown-piece, for the encouragement of national labour, James B. might have done himself. The stone has only been thrown upon one part of the lake, because the law has prevented it from being thrown upon another.

Therefore, that which is not seen supersedes that which is seen, and at this point there remains, as the residue of the operation, a piece of injustice, and, sad to say, a piece of injustice perpetrated by the law!

This is not all. I have said that there is always a third person left in the background. I must now bring him forward, that he may reveal to us a second loss of five francs. Then we shall have the entire results of the transaction.

James B. is the possessor of fifteen francs, the fruit of his labour. He is now free. What does he do with his fifteen francs? He purchases some article of fashion for ten francs, and with it he pays (or the intermediate pay for him) for the hundred-weight of Belgian iron. After this he has five francs left. He does not throw them into the river, but (and this is what is not seen) he gives them to some tradesman in exchange for some enjoyment; to a bookseller, for instance, for Bossuet's *Discourse on Universal History*.

Thus, as far as national labour is concerned, it is encouraged to the amount of fifteen francs, viz.: Ten francs for the Paris article; five francs to the bookselling trade.

As to James B., he obtains for his fifteen francs two gratifications, viz.:

1st. A hundred-weight of iron.
2nd. A book.

The decree is put in force. How does it affect the condition of James B.? How does it affect the national labour?

James B. pays every centime of his five francs to M. Prohibant, and therefore is deprived of the pleasure of a book, or of some other thing of equal value. He loses five francs. This must be admitted; it cannot fail to be admitted, that when the restriction raises the price of things, the consumer loses the difference.

But, then, it is said, national labour is the gainer.

No, it is not the gainer; for since the Act, it is no more encouraged than it was before, to the amount of fifteen francs.

The only thing is that, since the Act, the fifteen francs of James B. go to the metal trade, while before it was put in force, they were divided between the milliner and the bookseller.

The violence used by M. Prohibant on the frontier, or that which he causes to be used by the law, may be judged very differently in a moral point of view. Some persons consider that plunder is perfectly justifyable, if only sanctioned by law. But, for myself, I cannot imagine anything more aggravating. However it may be, the economical results are the same in both cases.

Look at the thing as you will; but if you are impartial, you will see that no good can come of legal or illegal plunder. We do not deny that it affords M. Prohibant, or his trade, or, if you will, national industry, a profit of five francs. But we affirm that it causes two losses, one to James B., who pays fifteen francs where he otherwise would have paid ten; the other to national industry, which does not receive the difference. Take your choice of these two losses, and compensate with it the profit which we allow. The other will prove not the less a dead loss. Here is the moral: To take by violence is not to produce, but to destroy. Truly, if taking by violence was producing, this country of ours would be a little richer than she is.

VIII. Machinery

"A curse on machines! Every year, their increasing power devotes millions of workmen to pauperism, by depriving them of work, and therefore of wages and bread. A curse on machines!"

This is the cry which is raised by vulgar prejudice, and echoed in the journals.

But to curse machines is to curse the spirit of humanity!

It puzzles me to conceive how any man can feel any satisfaction in such a doctrine.

For, if true, what is its inevitable consequence? That there is no activity, prosperity, wealth, or happiness possible for any people, except for those who are stupid and inert, and to whom God has not granted the fatal gift of knowing how to think, to observe, to combine, to invent, and to obtain the greatest results with the smallest means. On the contrary, rags, mean huts, poverty, and inanition, are the inevitable lot of every nation which seeks and finds in iron, fire, wind, electricity, magnetism, the laws of chemistry and mechanics, in a word, in the powers of nature, an assistance to its natural powers. We might as well say with Rousseau—"Every man that thinks is a depraved animal."

This is not all. If this doctrine is true, since all men think and invent, since all, from first to last, and at every moment of their existence, seek the cooperation of the powers of nature, and try to make the most of a little, by reducing either the work of their hands or their expenses, so as to obtain the greatest possible amount of gratification with the smallest possible amount of labour, it must follow, as a matter of course, that the whole of mankind is rushing towards its decline, by the same mental aspiration towards progress, which torments each of its members.

Hence, it ought to be made known, by statistics, that the inhabitants of Lancashire, abandoning that land of machines, seek for work in Ireland, where they are unknown; and, by history, that barbarism darkens the epochs of civilization, and that civilization shines in times of ignorance and barbarism.

There is evidently in this mass of contradictions something which revolts us, and which leads us to suspect that the problem contains within it an element of solution which has not been sufficiently disengaged.

Here is the whole mystery: Behind that which is seen lies something which is not seen. I will endeavor to bring it to light. The demonstration I shall give will only be a repetition of the preceding one, for the problems are one and the same.

Men have a natural propensity to make the best bargain they can, when not prevented by an opposing force; that is, they like to obtain as much as they possibly can for their labour, whether the advantage is obtained from a foreign producer or a skilful mechanical producer.

The theoretical objection which is made to this propensity is the same in both cases. In each case it is reproached with the apparent inactivity which it causes to labour. Now, labour rendered available, not inactive, is the very thing which determines it. And, therefore, in both cases, the same practical obstacle—force, is opposed to it also.

The legislator prohibits foreign competition, and forbids mechanical competition. For what other means can exist for arresting a propensity which is natural to all men, but that of depriving them of their liberty?

In many countries, it is true, the legislator strikes at only one of these competitions, and confines himself to grumbling at the other. This only proves one thing, that is, that the legislator is inconsistent.

We need not be surprised at this. On a wrong road, inconsistency is inevitable; if it were not so, mankind would be sacrificed. A false principle never has been, and never will be, carried out to the end.

Now for our demonstration, which shall not be a long one.

James B. had two francs which he had gained by two workmen; but it occurs to him that an arrangement of ropes and weights might be made which would diminish the labour by half. Therefore he obtains the same advantage, saves a franc, and discharges a workman.

He discharges a workman: this is that which is seen.

And seeing this only, it is said, "See how misery attends civilization; this is the way that liberty is fatal to equality. The human mind has made a conquest, and immediately a workman is cast into the gulf of pauperism. James B. may possibly employ the two workmen, but then he will give them only half their wages, for they will compete with each other, and offer themselves at the lowest price. Thus, the rich are always growing richer, and the poor, poorer. Society wants remodeling." A very fine conclusion, and worthy of the preamble.

Happily, preamble and conclusion are both false, because, behind the half of the phenomenon which is seen, lies the other half which is not seen.

The franc saved by James B. is not seen, no more are the necessary effects of this saving.

Since, in consequence of his invention, James B. spends only one franc on hand labour in the pursuit of a determined advantage, another franc remains to him.

If, then, there is in the world a workman with unemployed arms, there is also in the world a capitalist with an unemployed franc. These two elements meet and combine, and it is as clear as daylight, that between the supply and demand of labour, and between the supply and demand of wages, the relation is in no way changed.

The invention and the workman paid with the first franc, now perform the work which was formerly accomplished by two workmen. The second workman, paid with the second franc, realizes a new kind of work.

What is the change, then, which has taken place? An additional national advantage has been gained; in other words, the invention is a gratuitous triumph—a gratuitous profit for mankind.

From the form which I have given to my demonstration, the following inference might be drawn: "It is the capitalist who reaps all the advantage from machinery. The working class, if it suffers only temporarily, never profits by it, since, by your own showing, they displace a portion of the national labour, without diminishing it, it is true, but also without increasing it."

I do not pretend, in this slight treatise, to answer every objection; the only end I have in view, is to combat a vulgar, widely spread, and dangerous prejudice. I want to prove that a new machine only causes the discharge of a certain number of hands, when the remuneration which pays them is abstracted by force. These hands and this remuneration would combine to produce what it was impossible to produce before the invention; whence it follows, that the final result is an increase of advantages for equal labour.

Who is the gainer by these additional advantages?

First, it is true, the capitalist, the inventor; the first who succeeds in using the machine; and this is the reward of his genius and courage. In this case, as we have just seen, he effects a saving upon the expense of production, which, in whatever way it may be spent (and it always is spent), employs exactly as many hands as the machine caused to be dismissed.

But soon competition obliges him to lower his prices in proportion to the saving itself; and then it is no longer the inventor who reaps the benefit of the invention—it is the purchaser of what is produced, the consumer, the public, including the workman; in a word, mankind.

And that which is not seen is, that the saving thus procured for all consumers creates a fund whence wages may be supplied, and which replaces that which the machine has exhausted.

Thus, to recur to the forementioned example, James B. obtains a profit by spending two francs in wages. Thanks to his invention, the hand labour costs him only one franc. So long as he sells the thing produced at the same price, he employs one workman less in producing this particular thing, and that is what is seen; but there is an additional workman employed by the franc which James B. has saved. This is that which is not seen.

When, by the natural progress of things, James B. is obliged to lower the price of the thing produced by one franc, then he no longer realizes a saving; then he has no longer a franc to dispose of to procure for the national labour a new production. But then another gainer takes his place, and this gainer is mankind. Whoever buys the thing he has produced, pays a franc less, and necessarily adds this saving to the fund of wages; and this, again, is what is not seen.

Another solution, founded upon facts, has been given of this problem of machinery.

It was said, machinery reduces the expense of production, and lowers the price of the thing produced. The reduction of the profit causes an increase of consumption, which necessitates an increase of production; and, finally, the introduction of as many workmen, or more, after the invention as were necessary before it. As a proof of this, printing, weaving, etc., are instanced.

This demonstration is not a scientific one. It would lead us to conclude, that if the consumption of the particular production of which we are speaking remains stationary, or nearly so, machinery must injure labour. This is not the case.

Suppose that in a certain country all the people wore hats. If, by machinery, the price could be reduced half, it would not necessarily follow that the consumption would be doubled.

Would you say that in this case a portion of the national labour had been paralyzed? Yes, according to the vulgar demonstration; but, according to mine, No; for even if not a single hat more should be bought in the country, the entire fund of wages would not be the less secure. That which failed to go to the hat-making trade would be found to have gone to the economy realized by all the consumers, and would thence serve to pay for all the labour which the machine had rendered useless, and to excite a new development of all the trades. And thus it is that things go on. I have known newspapers to cost eighty francs, now we pay forty-eight: here is a saving of thirty-two francs to the subscribers. It is not certain, or at least necessary, that the thirty-two francs should take the direction of the journalist trade; but it is certain, and necessary too, that if they do not take this direction they will take another. One makes use of them for taking in more newspapers; another, to get better living; another, better clothes; another, better furniture. It is thus that the trades are bound together. They form a vast whole, whose different parts communicate by secret canals; what is saved by one, profits all. It is very important for us to understand that savings never take place at the expense of labour and wages.

IX. Credit

In all times, but more especially of late years, attempts have been made to extend wealth by the extension of credit.

I believe it is no exaggeration to say, that since the revolution of February, the Parisian presses have issued more than ten thousand pamphlets, crying up this solution of the social problem. The only basis, alas! of this solution, is an optical delusion—if, indeed, an optical delusion can be called a basis at all.

The first thing done is to confuse cash with produce, then paper money with cash; and from these two confusions it is pretended that a reality can be drawn.

It is absolutely necessary in this question to forget money, coin, bills, and the other instruments by means of which productions pass from hand to hand. Our business is with the productions themselves, which are the real objects of the loan; for when a farmer borrows fifty francs to buy a plough, it is not, in reality, the fifty francs which are lent to him, but the plough; and when a merchant borrows twenty thousand francs to purchase a house, it is not the twenty thousand francs which he owes, but the house. Money only appears for the sake of facilitating the arrangements between the parties.

Peter may not be disposed to lend his plough, but James may be willing to lend his money. What does William do in this case? He borrows money of James, and with this money he buys the plough of Peter.

But, in point of fact, no one borrows money for the sake of the money itself; money is only the medium by which to obtain possession of productions. Now, it is impossible in any country to transmit from one person to another more productions than that country contains.

Whatever may be the amount of cash and of paper which is in circulation, the whole of the borrowers cannot receive more ploughs, houses, tools, and supplies of raw material, than the lenders altogether can furnish; for we must take care not to forget that every borrower supposes a lender, and that what is once borrowed implies a loan.

This granted, what advantage is there in institutions of credit? It is, that they facilitate, between borrowers and lenders, the means of finding and treating with each other; but it is not in their power to cause an instantaneous increase of the things to be borrowed and lent. And yet they ought to be able to do so, if the aim of the reformers is to be attained, since they aspire to nothing less than to place ploughs, houses, tools, and provisions in the hands of all those who desire them.

And how do they intend to effect this?

By making the State security for the loan.

Let us try and fathom the subject, for it contains something which is seen, and also something which is not seen. We must endeavor to look at both.

We will suppose that there is but one plough in the world, and that two farmers apply for it.

Peter is the possessor of the only plough which is to be had in France; John and James wish to borrow it. John, by his honesty, his property, and good reputation, offers security. He inspires confidence; he has *credit*. James inspires little or no confidence. It naturally happens that Peter lends his plough to John.

But now, according to the Socialist plan, the State interferes, and says to Peter, "Lend your plough to James, I will be security for its return, and this security will be better than that of John, for he has no one to be responsible for him but himself; and I, although it is true that I have nothing, dispose of the fortune of the tax-payers, and it is with their money that, in case of need, I shall pay you the principal and interest." Consequently, Peter lends his plough to James; this is what is seen.

And the Socialists rub their hands, and say, "See how well our plan has answered. Thanks to the intervention of the State, poor James has a plough. He will no longer be obliged to dig the ground; he is on the road to make a fortune. It is a good thing for him, and an advantage to the nation as a whole."

Indeed, it is no such thing; it is no advantage to the nation, for there is something behind which is not seen.

It is not seen, that the plough is in the hands of James, only because it is not in those of John.

It is not seen, that if James farms instead of digging, John will be reduced to the necessity of digging instead of farming.

156

That, consequently, what was considered an increase of loan, is nothing but a displacement of loan. Besides, it is not seen that this displacement implies two acts of deep injustice.

It is an injustice to John, who, after having deserved and obtained credit by his honesty and activity, sees himself robbed of it.

It is an injustice to the tax-payers, who are made to pay a debt which is no concern of theirs.

Will any one say, that government offers the same facilities to John as it does to James? But as there is only one plough to be had, two cannot be lent. The argument always maintains that, thanks to the intervention of the State, more will be borrowed than there are things to be lent; for the plough represents here the bulk of available capitals.

It is true, I have reduced the operation to the most simple expression of it, but if you submit the most complicated government institutions of credit to the same test, you will be convinced that they can have but one result; viz., to displace credit, not to augment it. In one country, and in a given time, there is only a certain amount of capital available, and all are employed. In guaranteeing the non-payers, the State may, indeed, increase the number of borrowers, and thus raise the rate of interest (always to the prejudice of the tax-payer), but it has no power to increase the number of lenders, and the importance of the total of the loans.

There is one conclusion, however, which I would not for the world be suspected of drawing. I say, that the law ought not to favour, artificially, the power of borrowing, but I do not say that it ought not to restrain them artificially. If, in our system of mortgage, or in any other, there be obstacles to the diffusion of the application of credit, let them be got rid of; nothing can be better or more just than this. But this is all which is consistent with liberty, and it is all that any who are worthy of the name of reformers will ask.

X. Algeria

Here are four orators disputing for the platform. First, all the four speak at once; then they speak one after the other. What have they said? Some very fine things, certainly, about the power and the grandeur of France; about the necessity of sowing, if we would reap; about the brilliant future of our gigantic colony; about the advantage of diverting to a distance the surplus of our population, etc. Magnificent pieces of eloquence, and always adorned with this conclusion: "Vote fifty millions, more or less, for making ports and roads in Algeria; for sending emigrants thither; for building houses and breaking up land. By so doing, you will relieve the French workman, encourage African labour, and give a stimulus to the commerce of Marseilles. It would be profitable every way."

Yes, it is all very true, if you take no account of the fifty millions until the moment when the State begins to spend them; if you only see where they go, and not whence they come; if you look only at the good they are to do when they come out of the tax-gatherer's bag, and not at the harm which has been done, and the good which has been prevented, by putting them into it. Yes, at this limited point of view, all is profit. The house which is built in Barbary is that which is seen; the harbour made in Barbary is that which is seen; the work caused in Barbary is what is seen; a few less hands in France is what is seen; a great stir with goods at Marseilles is still that which is seen.

But, besides all this, there is something which is not seen. The fifty millions expended by the State cannot be spent, as they otherwise would have been, by the tax-payers. It is necessary to deduct, from all the good attributed to the public expenditure which has been effected, all the harm caused by the prevention of private expense, unless we say that James B. would have done nothing with the crown that he had gained, and of which the tax had deprived him; an absurd assertion, for if he took the trouble to earn it, it was because he expected the satisfaction of using it. He would have repaired the palings in his garden, which he cannot now do, and this is that which is not seen. He would have manured his field, which now he cannot do, and this is what is not seen. He would have added another story to his cottage, which he cannot do now, and this is what is not seen. He might have increased the number of his tools, which he cannot do now, and this is what is not seen. He would have been better fed, better clothed, have given a better education to his children, and increased his daughter's marriage portion; this is what is not seen. He would have become a member of the Mutual Assistance Society, but now he cannot; this is what is not seen. On one hand, are the enjoyments of which he has been deprived, and the means of action which have been destroyed in his hands; on the other, are the labour of the drainer, the carpenter, the smith, the tailor, the village schoolmaster, which he would have encouraged, and which are now prevented—all this is what is not seen.

Much is hoped from the future prosperity of Algeria; be it so. But the drain to which France is being subjected ought not to be kept entirely out of sight. The commerce of Marseilles is pointed out to me; but if this is to be brought about by means of taxation, I shall always show that an equal commerce is destroyed thereby in other parts of the country. It is said, "There is an emigrant transported into Barbary; this is a relief to the population which remains in the country." I answer, "How can that be, if, in transporting this emigrant to Algiers, you also transport two or three times the capital which would have served to maintain him in France?"[1]

The only object I have in view is to make it evident to the reader, that in every public expense, behind the apparent benefit, there is an evil which it is not so easy to discern. As far as in me lies, I would make him form a habit of seeing both, and taking account of both.

When a public expense is proposed, it ought to be examined in itself, separately from the pretended encouragement of labour which results from it, for this encouragement is a delusion. Whatever is done in this way at the public expense, private expense would have done all the same; therefore, the interest of labour is always out of the question.

It is not the object of this treatise to criticize the intrinsic merit of the public expenditure as applied to Algeria, but I cannot withhold a general observation. It is, that the presumption is always unfavourable to collective expenses by way of tax. Why? For this reason: First, justice always suffers from it in some degree. Since James B. had laboured to gain his crown, in the hope of receiving a gratification from it, it is to be regretted that the exchequer should interpose, and take from James B. this gratification, to bestow it upon another. Certainly, it behooves the exchequer, or those who regulate it, to give good reasons for this. It has been shown that the State gives a very provoking one, when it says, "With this crown I shall employ workmen;" for James B. (as soon as he sees it) will be sure to answer, "It is all very fine, but with this crown I might employ them myself."

Apart from this reason, others present themselves without disguise, by which the debate between the exchequer and poor James becomes much simplified. If the State says to him, "I take your crown to pay the gendarme, who saves you the trouble of providing for your own personal safety; for paving the street which you are passing through every day; for paying the magistrate who causes your property and your liberty to be respected; to maintain the soldier who maintains our frontiers,"—James B., unless I am much mistaken, will pay for all this without hesitation. But if the State were to say to him, "I take this crown that I may give you a little prize in case you cultivate your field well; or that I may teach your son something that you have no wish that he should learn; or that the Minister may add another to his score of dishes at dinner; I take it to build a cottage in Algeria, in which case I must take another crown every year to keep an emigrant in it, and another hundred to maintain a soldier to guard this emigrant, and another crown to maintain a general to guard this soldier," etc.,—I think I hear poor James exclaim, "This system of law is very much like a system of cheat!" The State foresees the objection, and what does it do? It jumbles all things together, and brings forward just that provoking reason which ought to have nothing whatever to do with the question. It talks of the effect of this crown upon labour; it points to the cook and purveyor of the Minister; it shows an emigrant, a soldier, and a general, living upon the crown; it shows, in fact, what is seen, and if James B. has not learned to take into the account what is not seen, James B. will be duped. And this is why I want to do all I can to impress it upon his mind, by repeating it over and over again.

As the public expenses displace labour without increasing it, a second serious presumption presents itself against them. To displace labour is to displace labourers, and to disturb the natural laws which regulate the distribution of the population over the country. If fifty millions francs are allowed to remain in the possession of the tax-payers since the tax-payers are everywhere, they encourage labour in the forty thousand parishes in France. They act like a natural tie, which keeps every one upon his native soil; they distribute themselves amongst all imaginable labourers and trades. If the State, by drawing off these fifty millions francs from the citizens, accumulates them, and expends them on some given point, it attracts to this point a proportional quantity of displaced labour, a corresponding number of labourers, belonging to other parts; a fluctuating population, which is out of its place, and I venture to say dangerous when the fund is exhausted. Now here is the consequence (and this confirms all I have said): this feverish activity is, as it were, forced into a narrow space; it attracts the attention of all; it is what is seen. The people applaud; they are astonished at the beauty and facility of the plan, and expect to have it continued and extended. That which they do not see is, that an equal quantity of labour, which would probably be more valuable, has been paralyzed over the rest of France.

XI. Frugality and Luxury

It is not only in the public expenditure that what is seen eclipses what is not seen. Setting aside what relates to political economy, this phenomenon leads to false reasoning. It causes nations to consider their moral and their material interests as contradictory to each other. What can be more discouraging, or more dismal?

For instance, there is not a father of a family who does not think it his duty to teach his children order, system, the habits of carefulness, of economy, and of moderation in spending money.

There is no religion which does not thunder against pomp and luxury. This is as it should be; but, on the other hand, how frequently do we hear the following remarks:

"To hoard, is to drain the veins of the people."

"The luxury of the great is the comfort of the little."

"Prodigals ruin themselves, but they enrich the State."

"It is the superfluity of the rich which makes bread for the poor."

Here, certainly, is a striking contradiction between the moral and the social idea. How many eminent spirits, after having made the assertion, repose in peace. It is a thing I never could understand, for it seems to me that nothing can be more distressing than to discover two opposite tendencies in mankind. Why, it comes to degradation at each of the extremes; economy brings it to misery; prodigality plunges it into moral degradation. Happily, these vulgar maxims exhibit economy and luxury in a false light, taking account, as they do, of those immediate consequences *which are seen,* and not of the remote ones, which are not seen. Let us see if we can rectify this incomplete view of the case.

Mondor and his brother Aristus, after dividing the parental inheritance, have each an income of fifty thousand francs. Mondor practices the fashionable philanthropy. He is what is called a squanderer of money. He renews his furniture several times a year; changes his equipages every month. People talk of his ingenious contrivances to bring them sooner to an end: In short, he surpasses the fast livers of Balzac and Alexander Dumas.

Thus, everybody is singing his praises. It is, "Tell us about Mondor! Mondor for ever! He is the benefactor of the workman; a blessing to the people. It is true, he revels in dissipation; he splashes the passers-by; his own dignity and that of human nature are lowered a little; but what of that? He does good with his fortune, if not with himself. He causes money to circulate; he always sends the tradespeople away satisfied. Is not money made round that it may roll?"

Aristus has adopted a very different plan of life. If he is not an egotist, he is, at any rate, an individualist, for he considers expense, seeks only moderate and reasonable enjoyments, thinks of his children's prospects, and, in fact, he economizes.

And what do people say of him? "What is the good of a rich fellow like him? He is a skinflint. There is something imposing, perhaps, in the simplicity of his life; and he is humane, too, and benevolent, and generous, but he calculates. He does not spend his income; his house is neither brilliant nor bustling. What good does he do to the paper hangers, the carriage makers, the horse dealers, and the confectioners?"

These opinions, which are fatal to morality, are founded upon what strikes the eye: The expenditure of the prodigal; and another, which is out of sight, the equal and even superior expenditure of the economist.

But things have been so admirably arranged by the Divine inventor of social order, that in this, as in everything else, political economy and morality, far from clashing, agree; and the wisdom of Aristus is not only more dignified, but still more profitable, than the folly of Mondor. And when I say profitable, I do not mean only profitable to Aristus, or even to society in general, but more profitable to the workmen themselves—to the trade of the time.

To prove it, it is only necessary to turn the mind's eye to those hidden consequences of human actions, which the bodily eye does not see.

Yes, the prodigality of Mondor has visible effects in every point of view. Everybody can see his landaus, his phaetons, his berlins, the delicate paintings on his ceilings, his rich carpets, the brilliant effects of his house. Every one knows that his horses run upon the turf. The dinners which he gives at the Hotel de Paris attract the attention of the crowds on the Boulevards; and it is said, "That is a generous man; far from saving his income, he is very likely breaking into his capital." That is what is seen.

It is not so easy to see, with regard to the interest of workers, what becomes of the income of Aristus. If we were to trace it carefully, however, we should see that the whole of it, down to the last farthing, affords work to the labourers, as certainly as the fortune of Mondor. Only there is this difference: The wanton extravagance of Mondor is doomed to be constantly decreasing, and to come to an end without fail; whilst the wise expenditure of Aristus will go on increasing from year to year. And if this is the case, then, most assuredly, the public interest will be in unison with morality.

Aristus spends upon himself and his household twenty thousand francs a year. If that is not sufficient to content him, he does not deserve to be called a wise man. He is touched by the miseries which oppress the poorer classes; he thinks he is bound in conscience to afford them some relief, and therefore he devotes ten thousand francs to acts of benevolence. Amongst the merchants, the manufacturers, and the agriculturists, he has friends who are suffering under temporary difficulties; he makes himself acquainted with their situation, that he may assist them with prudence and efficiency, and to this work he devotes ten thousand francs more. Then he does not forget that he has daughters to portion, and sons for whose prospects it is his duty to provide, and therefore he considers it a duty to lay by and put out to interest ten thousand francs every year.

The following is a list of his expenses:
1st, Personal expenses . . . . . 20,000 fr.
2nd, Benevolent objects 10,000
3rd, Offices of friendship . . . 10,000
4th, Saving 10,000

Let us examine each of these items, and we shall see that not a single farthing escapes the national labour.

1st. Personal expenses.—These, as far as workpeople and tradesmen are concerned, have precisely the same effect as an equal sum spent by Mondor. This is self-evident, therefore we shall say no more about it.

2nd. Benevolent objects.—The ten thousand francs devoted to this purpose benefit trade in an equal degree; they reach the butcher, the baker, the tailor, and the carpenter. The only thing is, that the bread, the meat, and the clothing are not used by Aristus, but by those whom he has made his substitutes. Now, this simple substitution of one consumer for another in no way affects trade in general. It is all one, whether Aristus spends a crown or desires some unfortunate person to spend it instead.

3rd. Offices of friendship.—The friend to whom Aristus lends or gives ten thousand francs does not receive them to bury them; that would be against the hypothesis. He uses them to pay for goods, or to discharge debts. In the first case, trade is encouraged. Will any one pretend to say that it gains more by Mondor's purchase of a thoroughbred horse for ten thousand francs than by the purchase of ten thousand francs' worth of stuffs by Aristus or his friend? For if this sum serves to pay a debt, a third person appears, viz., the creditor, who will certainly employ them upon something in his trade, his household, or his farm. He forms another medium between Aristus and the workmen. The names only are changed, the expense remains, and also the encouragement to trade.

4th. Saving.—There remains now the ten thousand francs saved; and it is here, as regards the encouragement to the arts, to trade, labour, and the workmen, that Mondor appears far superior to Aristus, although, in a moral point of view, Aristus shows himself, in some degree, superior to Mondor.

I can never look at these apparent contradictions between the great laws of nature without a feeling of physical uneasiness which amounts to suffering. Were mankind reduced to the necessity of choosing between two parties, one of whom injures his interest, and the other his conscience, we should have nothing to hope from the future. Happily, this is not the case; and to see Aristus regain his economical superiority, as well as his moral superiority, it is sufficient to understand this consoling maxim, which is no less true from having a paradoxical appearance, "To save is to spend."

What is Aristus' object in saving ten thousand francs? Is it to bury them in his garden? No, certainly; he intends to increase his capital and his income; consequently, this money, instead of being employed upon his own personal gratification, is used for buying land, a house, etc., or it is placed in the hands of a merchant or a banker. Follow the progress of this money in any one of these cases, and you will be convinced, that through the medium of vendors or lenders, it is encouraging labour quite as certainly as if Aristus, following the example of his brother, had exchanged it for furniture, jewels, and horses.

For when Aristus buys lands or rents for ten thousand francs, he is determined by the consideration that he does not want to spend this money. This is why you complain of him.

But, at the same time, the man who sells the land or the rent, is determined by the consideration that he does want to spend the ten thousand francs in some way; so that the money is spent in any case, either by Aristus or by others in his stead.

With respect to the working class, to the encouragement of labour, there is only one difference between the conduct of Aristus and that of Mondor. Mondor spends the money himself, and around him, and therefore the effect is seen. Aristus, spending it partly through inter-mediate parties, and at a distance, the effect is not seen. But, in fact, those who know how to attribute effects to their proper causes, will perceive, that what is not seen is as certain as what is seen. This is proved by the fact, that in both cases the money circulates, and does not lie in the iron chest of the wise man, any more than it does in that of the spendthrift. It is, therefore, false to say that economy does actual harm to trade; as described above, it is equally beneficial with luxury.

But how far superior is it, if, instead of confining our thoughts to the present moment, we let them embrace a longer period!

Ten years pass away. What is become of Mondor and his fortune, and his great popularity? Mondor is ruined. Instead of spending sixty thousand francs every year in the social body, he is, perhaps, a burden to it. In any case, he is no longer the delight of shopkeepers; he is no longer the patron of the arts and of trade; he is no longer of any use to the workmen, nor are his successors, whom he has brought to want.

At the end of the same ten years Aristus not only continues to throw his income into circulation, but he adds an increasing sum from year to year to his expenses. He enlarges the national capital, that is, the fund which supplies wages, and as it is upon the extent of this fund that the demand for hands depends, he assists in progressively increasing the remuneration of the working class; and if he dies, he leaves children whom he has taught to succeed him in this work of progress and civilization.

In a moral point of view, the superiority of frugality over luxury is indisputable. It is consoling to think that it is so in political economy, to every one who, not confining his views to the immediate effects of phe-nomena, knows how to extend his investigations to their final effects.

XII. He Who Has a Right to Work, Has a Right to Profit

"Brethren, you must club together to find me work at your own price." This is the right to work; i.e., elementary socialism of the first degree.

"Brethren, you must club together to find me work at my own price." This is the right to profit; i.e., refined socialism, or socialism of the second degree.

Both of these live upon such of their effects as are seen. They will die by means of those effects which are not seen.

That which is seen is the labour and the profit excited by social combination. That which is not seen is the labour and the profit to which this same combination would give rise, if it were left to the tax-payers.

In 1848, the right to labour for a moment showed two faces. This was sufficient to ruin it in public opinion.

One of these faces was called *national workshops*. The other, *forty-five centimes*. Millions of francs went daily from the Rue Rivoli to the national workshops. This was the fair side of the medal.

And this is the reverse. If millions are taken out of a cash-box, they must first have been put into it. This is why the organizers of the right to public labour apply to the tax-payers.

Now, the peasants said, "I must pay forty-five centimes; then I must deprive myself of some clothing. I cannot manure my field; I cannot repair my house."

And the country workmen said, "As our townsman deprives himself of some clothing, there will be less work for the tailor; as he does not improve his field, there will be less work for the drainer; as he does not repair his house, there will be less work for the carpenter and mason."

It was then proved that two kinds of meal cannot come out of one sack, and that the work furnished by the government was done at the expense of labour, paid for by the tax-payer. This was the death of the right to labour, which showed itself as much a chimera as an injustice. And yet, the right to profit, which is only an exaggeration of the right to labour, is still alive and flourishing.

Ought not the protectionist to blush at the part he would make society play?

He says to it, "You must give me work, and, more than that, lucrative work. I have foolishly fixed upon a trade by which I lose ten per cent. If you impose a tax of twenty francs upon my countrymen, and give it to me, I shall be a gainer instead of a loser. Now, profit is my right; you owe it me." Now, any society which would listen to this sophist, burden itself with taxes to satisfy him, and not perceive that the loss to which any trade is exposed is no less a loss when others are forced to make up for it, such a society, I say, would deserve the burden inflicted upon it.

Thus we learn by the numerous subjects which I have treated, that, to be ignorant of political economy is to allow ourselves to be dazzled by the immediate effect of a phenomenon; to be acquainted with it is to embrace in thought and in forethought the whole compass of effects.

I might subject a host of other questions to the same test; but I shrink from the monotony of a constantly uniform demonstration, and I conclude by applying to political economy what Chateaubriand says of history:

"There are," he says, "two consequences in history; an immediate one, which is instantly recognized, and one in the distance, which is not at first perceived. These consequences often contradict each other; the former are the results of our own limited wisdom, the latter, those of that wisdom which endures. The providential event appears after the human event. God rises up behind men. Deny, if you will, the supreme counsel; disown its action; dispute about words; designate, by the term, force of circumstances, or reason, what the vulgar call Providence; but look to the end of an accomplished fact, and you will see that it has always produced the contrary of what was expected from it, if it was not established at first upon morality and justice."—*Chateaubriand's Posthumous Memoirs*.

Notes

1. The Minister of War has lately asserted, that every individual transported to Algeria has cost the State eight thousand francs. Now it is certain that these poor creatures could have lived very well in France on a capital of four thousand francs. I ask, how the French population is relieved, when it is deprived of a man, and of the means of subsistence of two men?

Essays on Some Unsettled Questions of Political Economy
Essay IV: On Profits, and Interest

John Stuart Mill; 1844

The profits of stock are the surplus which remains to the capitalist after replacing his capital; and the ratio which that surplus bears to the capital itself, is the *rate* of profit.

This being the definition of profits, it might seem natural to adopt, as a sufficient theory in regard to the rate of profit, that it depends upon the productive power of capital. Some countries are favoured beyond others, either by nature or art, in the means of production. If the powers of the soil, or of machinery, enable capital to produce what is necessary for replacing itself, and twenty per cent more, profits will be twenty per cent; and so on.

This, accordingly, is a popular mode of speaking on the subject of profits; but it has only the semblance, not the reality, of an explanation. The "productive power of capital," though a common, and, for some purposes, a convenient expression, is a delusive one. Capital, strictly speaking, has no productive power. The only productive power is that of labour; assisted, no doubt, by tools, and acting upon materials. That portion of capital which consists of tools and materials, may be said, perhaps, without any great impropriety, to have a productive power, because they contribute, along with labour, to the accomplishment of production. But that portion of capital which consists of wages, has no productive power of its own. Wages have no productive power; they are the price of a productive power. Wages do not contribute, along with labour, to the production of commodities, no more than the price of tools contributes along with the tools themselves. If labour could be had without purchase, wages might be dispensed with. That portion of capital which is expended in the wages of labour, is only the means by which the capitalist procures to himself, in the way of purchase, the use of that labour in which the power of production really resides.

The proper view of capital is, that anything whatever, which a person possesses, constitutes his capital, provided he is able, and intends, to employ it, not in consumption for the purpose of enjoyment, but in possessing himself of the means of production, with the intention of employing those means productively. Now the means of production are labour, implements, and materials. The only productive power which anywhere exists, is the productive power of labour, implements, and materials.

We need not, on this account, altogether proscribe the expression, "productive power of capital;" but we should carefully note, that it can only mean the quantity of real productive power which the capitalist, by means of his capital, can command. This may change, though the productive power of labour remains the same. Wages, for example, may rise; and then, although all the circumstances of production remain exactly as they were before, the same capital will yield a less return, because it will set in motion a less quantity of productive labour.

We may, therefore, consider the capital of a producer as measured by the means which he has of possessing himself of the different essentials of production: namely, labour, and the various articles which labour requires as materials, or of which it avails itself as aids. The ratio between the price which he has to pay for these means of production, and the produce which they enable him to raise, is the *rate* of his profit. If he must give for labour and tools four-fifths of what they will produce, the remaining fifth will constitute his profit, and will give him a rate of one in four, or twenty-five per cent, on his outlay.

It is necessary here to remark, what cannot indeed by any possibility be misunderstood, but might possibly be overlooked in cases where attention to it is indispensable, viz., that we are speaking now of the *rate* of profit, not the gross profit. If the capital of the country is very great, a profit of only five per cent upon it may be much more ample, may support a much larger number of capitalists and their families in much greater affluence, than a profit of twenty-five per cent on the comparatively small capital of a poor country. The *gross* profit of a country is the actual amount of necessaries, conveniences, and luxuries, which are divided among its capitalists: But whether this be large or small, the rate of profit may be just the same. The rate of profit is the proportion which the profit bears to the capital; which the surplus produce after replacing the outlay, bears to the outlay. In short, if we compare the *price* paid for labour and tools with what that labour and those tools will *produce,* from this ratio we may calculate the rate of profit.

As the gross profit may be very different though the rate of profit be the same; so also may the absolute price paid for labour and tools be very different, and yet the proportion between the price paid and the produce obtained may be just the same. For greater clearness, let us omit, for the present, the consideration of tools, materials, etc., and conceive production as the result solely of labour. In a certain country, let us suppose, the wages of each labourer are one quarter of wheat per year, and one hundred men can produce, in one year, one hundred and twenty quarters. Here the price paid for labour is to the produce of that labour as one hundred to one hundred and twenty, and profits are twenty per cent. Suppose now that, in another country, wages are just double what they are in the country before supposed; namely, two quarters of wheat per year, for each labourer. But suppose, likewise, that the productive power of labour is double what it is in the first country; that by the greater fertility of the soil, one hundred men can produce two hundred and forty quarters, instead of one hundred and twenty as before. Here it is obvious, that the real price paid for labour is twice as great in the one country as in the other; but the produce being also twice as great, the ratio between the price of labour and the produce of labour is still exactly the same: An outlay of two hundred quarters gives a return of two hundred and forty quarters, and profits, as before, are twenty per cent.

Profits, then (meaning not gross profits, but the rate of profit), depend not upon the price of labour, tools, and materials—but upon the ratio between the price of labour, tools, and materials, and the produce of them; upon the proportionate share of the produce of industry which it is necessary to offer, in order to purchase that industry and the means of setting it in motion.

We have hitherto spoken of tools, buildings, and materials, as essentials of production, coordinate with labour, and equally indispensable with it. This is true; but it is also true that tools, buildings, and materials, are themselves the produce of labour; and that the only cause (cases of monopoly excepted) of their having any value, is the labour which is required for their production.

If tools, buildings, and materials were the spontaneous gifts of nature, requiring no labour either in order to produce or to appropriate them; and if they were thus bestowed upon mankind in indefinite quantity, and without the possibility of being monopolized; they would still be as useful, as indispensable as they now are; but since they could, like air and the light of the sun, be obtained without cost or sacrifice, they would form no part of the expenses of production, and no portion of the produce would be required to be set aside in order to replace the outlay made for these purposes. The whole produce, therefore, after replacing the wages of labour, would be clear profit to the capitalist.

Labour alone is the primary means of production; "the original purchase-money which has been paid for everything." Tools and materials, like other things, have originally cost nothing but labour; and have a value in the market only because wages have been paid for them. The labour employed in making the tools and materials being added to the labour afterwards employed in working up the materials by aid of the tools, the sum total gives the whole of the labour employed in the production of the completed commodity. In the ultimate analysis, therefore, labour appears to be the only essential of production. To replace capital, is to replace nothing but the wages of the labour employed. Consequently, the whole of the surplus, after replacing wages, is profits. From this it seems to follow, that the ratio between the wages of labour and the produce of that labour gives the rate of profit. And thus we arrive at Mr. Ricardo's principle, that profits depend upon wages; rising as wages fall, and falling as wages rise.

To protect this proposition (the most perfect form in which the law of profits seems to have been yet exhibited) against misapprehension, one or two explanatory remarks are required.

If by wages, be meant what constitutes the real affluence of the labourer, the *quantity* of produce which he receives in exchange for his labour; the proposition that profits vary inversely as wages, will be obviously false. The rate of profit (as has been already observed and exemplified) does not depend upon the price of labour, but upon the proportion between the price of labour and the produce of it. If the produce of labour is large, the price of labour may also be large without any diminution of the rate of profit: And, in fact, the rate of profit is highest in those countries (as, for instance, North America) where the labourer is most largely remunerated. For the wages of labour, though so large, bear a less proportion to the abundant *produce* of labour, there than elsewhere.

But this does not affect the truth of Mr. Ricardo's principle as he himself understood it; because an increase of the labourer's real comforts was not considered by him as a rise of wages. In his language, wages were only said to rise when they rose not in mere quantity but in *value.* To the labourer himself (he would have said) the *quantity* of his remuneration is the important circumstance: But its *value* is the only thing of importance to the person who purchases his labour.

The rate of profits depends not upon absolute or real wages, but upon the *value* of wages.

If, however, by value, Mr. Ricardo had meant *exchangeable* value, his proposition would still have been remote from the truth. Profits depend no more upon the exchangeable value of the labourer's remuneration, than upon its quantity. The truth is, that by the exchangeable value is meant the quantity of commodities which the labourer can purchase with his wages; so that when we say the exchangeable value of wages, we say their quantity, under another name.

Mr. Ricardo, however, did not use the word value in the sense of exchangeable value.

Occasionally, in his writings, he could not avoid using the word as other people use it, to denote value in exchange. But he more frequently employed it in a sense peculiar to himself, to denote cost of production; in other words, the *quantity of labour* required to produce the article; that being his criterion of cost of production. Thus, if a hat could be made with ten days' labour in France and with five days' labour in England, he said that the value of a hat was double in France of what it was in England. If a quarter of corn could be produced a century ago with half as much labour as is necessary at present, Mr. Ricardo said that the value of a quarter of corn had doubled.

Mr. Ricardo, therefore, would not have said that wages had risen, because a labourer could obtain two pecks of flour instead of one, for a day's labour; but if last year he received, for a day's labour, something which required eight hours' labour to produce it, and this year something which requires nine hours, then Mr. Ricardo would say that wages had risen. A rise of wages, with Mr. Ricardo, meant an increase in the cost of production of wages; an increase in the number of hours' labour which go to produce the wages of a day's labour; an increase in the *proportion* of the fruits of labour which the labourer receives for his own share; an increase in the ratio between the wages of his labour and the produce of it. This is the theory; the reasoning, of which it is the result, has been given in the preceding paragraphs.

Some of Mr. Ricardo's followers, or more properly, of those who have adopted in most particulars the views of political economy which his genius was the first to open up, have given explanations of Mr. Ricardo's doctrine to nearly the same effect as the above, but in rather different terms. They have said that profits depend not on *absolute,* but on *proportional* wages; which they expounded to mean the proportion which the labourers *en masse* receive of the total produce of the country.

It seems, however, to be rather an unusual and inconvenient use of language to speak of anything as depending upon the wages of labour, and then to explain that by wages of labour you do not mean the wages of an individual labourer, but of all the labourers in the country collectively. Mankind will never agree to call anything a rise of wages, except a rise of the wages of individual labourers, and it is therefore preferable to employ language tending to fix attention upon the wages of the individual. The wages, however, on which profits are said to depend, are undoubtedly *proportional* wages, namely, the proportional wages of one labourer: That is, the ratio between the wages of one labourer, and (not the whole produce of the country, but) the amount of what one labourer can produce; the amount of that portion of the collective produce of the industry of the country, which may be considered as corresponding to the labour of one single labourer. Proportional wages, thus understood, may be concisely termed the cost of production of wages; or, more concisely still, the cost of wages, meaning their cost in the "original purchase money," labour.

We have now arrived at a distinct conception of Mr. Ricardo's theory of profits in its most perfect state. And this theory we conceive to be the basis of the true theory of profits. All that remains to do is to clear it from certain difficulties which still surround it, and which, though in a greater degree apparent than real, are not to be put aside as wholly imaginary.

Though it is true that tools, materials, and buildings (it is to be wished that there were some compact designation for all these essentials of production taken together) are themselves the produce of labour, and are only on that account to be ranked among the expenses of production; yet the *whole* of their value is not resolvable into the wages of the labourers by whom they were produced. The wages of those labourers were paid by a capitalist, and that capitalist must have the same profit upon his advances as any other capitalist; when, therefore, he sells the tools or materials, he must receive from the purchaser not only the reimbursement of the wages he has paid, but also as much more as will afford him the ordinary rate of profit. And when the producer, after buying the tools and employing them in his own occupation, comes to estimate his gains, he must set aside a portion of the produce to replace not only the wages paid both by himself and by the tool maker, but also the profits of the tool maker, advanced by himself out of his own capital.

It is not correct, therefore, to state that all which the capitalist retains after replacing wages forms his profit. It is true the whole return to capital is either wages or profits; but profits do not compose merely the surplus after replacing the outlay; they also enter into the outlay itself. Capital is expended partly in paying or reimbursing wages, and partly in paying the profits of other capitalists, whose concurrence was necessary in order to bring together the means of production.

If any contrivance, therefore, were devised by which that part of the outlay which consists of previous profits could be either wholly or partially dispensed with, it is evident that more would remain as the profit of the immediate producer; while, as the quantity of *labour* necessary to produce a given quantity of the commodity would be unaltered, as well as the quantity of produce paid for that labour, it seems that the ratio between the price of labour and its produce would be the same as before; that the cost of production of wages would be the same, proportional wages the same, and yet profits different.

To illustrate this by a simple instance, let it be supposed that one third of the produce is sufficient to replace the wages of the labourers who have been immediately instrumental in the production; that another third is necessary to replace the materials used and the fixed capital worn out in the process; while the remaining third is clear gain, being a profit of fifty per cent. Suppose, for example, that sixty agricultural labourers, receiving sixty quarters of corn for their wages, consume fixed capital and seed amounting to the value of sixty quarters more, and that the result of their operations is a produce of one hundred and eighty quarters. When we analyze the price of the seed and tools into its elements, we find that they must have been the produce of the labour of forty men: For the wages of those forty, together with profit at the rate previously supposed (fifty per cent) make up sixty quarters. The produce, therefore, consisting of one hundred and eighty quarters, is the result of the labour altogether of one hundred men: namely, the sixty first mentioned, and the forty by whose labour the fixed capital and the seed were produced.

Let us now suppose, by way of an extreme case, that some contrivance is discovered, whereby the purposes to which the second third of the produce had been devoted, may be dispensed with altogether; that some means are invented by which the same amount of produce may be procured without the assistance of any fixed capital, or the consumption of any seed or material sufficiently valuable to be worth calculating. Let us, however, suppose that this cannot be done without taking on a number of additional labourers, equal to those required for producing the seed and fixed capital; so that the saving shall be only in the profits of the previous capitalists. Let us, in conformity with this supposition, assume that in dispensing with the fixed capital and seed, value sixty quarters, it is necessary to take on forty additional labourers, receiving a quarter of corn each, as before.

The rate of profit has evidently risen. It has increased from fifty per cent to eighty per cent. A return of one hundred and eighty quarters could not before be obtained but by an outlay of one hundred and twenty quarters; it can now be obtained by an outlay of no more than one hundred.

Here, therefore, is an undeniable rise of profits. Have wages, in the sense above attached to them, fallen or not? It would seem not.

The produce (one hundred and eighty quarters) is still the result of the same quantity of labour as before, namely, the labour of one hundred men. A quarter of corn, therefore, is still, as before, the produce of 10/18 of a man's labour for a year. Each labourer receives, as before, one quarter of corn; each, therefore, receives the produce of 10/18 of a year's labour of one man, that is, the same cost of production; each receives 10/18 of the produce of his own labour, that is, the same proportional wages; and the labourers collectively still receive the same proportion, namely 10/18, of the whole produce.

The conclusion, then, cannot be resisted, that Mr. Ricardo's theory is defective: That the rate of profits does *not* exclusively depend upon the value of wages, in his sense, namely, the quantity of labour of which the wages of a labourer are the produce; that it does *not* exclusively depend upon proportional wages, that is, upon the proportion which the labourers collectively receive of the whole produce, or the ratio which the wages of an individual labourer bear to the produce of his individual labour.

Those political economists, therefore, who have always dissented from Mr. Ricardo's doctrine, or who, having at first admitted, ended by discarding it, were so far in the right; but they committed a serious error in this, that, with the usual one-sidedness of disputants, they knew no medium between admitting absolutely and dismissing entirely; and saw no other course than utterly to reject what it would have been sufficient to modify.

It is remarkable how very slight a modification will suffice to render Mr. Ricardo's doctrine completely true. It is even doubtful whether he himself, if called upon to adapt his expressions to this peculiar case, would not have so explained his doctrine as to render it entirely unobjectionable.

It is perfectly true, that, in the example already made use of, a rise of profits takes place, while wages, considered in respect to the quantity of labour of which they are the produce, have not varied at all. But though wages are still the produce of the same *quantity of labour* as before, the *cost of production* of wages has nevertheless fallen; for into cost of production there enters another element besides labour.

We have already remarked (and the very example out of which the difficulty arose presupposes it) that the cost of production of an article consists generally of two parts—the *wages* of the labour employed, and the *profits* of those who, in any antecedent stage of the production, have advanced any portion of those wages. An article, therefore, may be the produce of the same quantity of labour as before, and yet, if any portion of the profits which the last producer has to make good to previous producers can be economized, the cost of production of the article is diminished.

Now, in our example, a diminution of this sort is supposed to have taken place in the cost of production of corn. The production of that article has become less costly, in the ratio of six to five. A quantity of corn, the means of producing which could not previously have been secured but at an expense of one hundred and twenty quarters, can now be produced by means which one hundred quarters are sufficient to purchase.

But the labourer is supposed to receive the same quantity of corn as before. He receives one quarter. The cost of production of wages has, therefore, fallen one sixth. A quarter of corn, which is the remuneration of a single labourer; is indeed the produce of the same quantity of labour as before; but its cost of production is nevertheless diminished. It is now the produce of 10/18 of a man's labour, and nothing else; whereas formerly it required for its production the conjunction of that quantity of labour with an expenditure, in the form of reimbursement of profit, amounting to one fifth more.

If the cost of production of wages had remained the same as before, profits could not have risen. Each labourer received one quarter of corn; but one quarter of corn at that time was the result of the same cost of production, as one and one fifth quarter now. In order, therefore, that each labourer should receive the same cost of production, each must now receive one quarter of corn, *plus* one fifth. The labour of one hundred men could not be purchased at this price for less than one hundred and twenty quarters; and the produce, one hundred and eighty quarters, would yield only fifty per cent, as first supposed.[1]

It is, therefore, strictly true, that the rate of profits varies inversely as the cost of production of wages. Profits cannot rise, unless the cost of production of wages falls exactly as much; nor fall, unless it rises.

The proof of this position has been stated in figures, and in a particular case: We shall now state it in general terms, and for all cases.

We have supposed, for simplicity, that wages are paid in the finished commodity. The agricultural labourers, in our example, were paid in corn, and if we had called them weavers, we should have supposed them to be paid in cloth. This supposition is allowable, for it is obviously of no consequence, in a question of value, or cost of production, what precise article we assume as the medium of exchange. The supposition has, besides, the recommendation of being conformable to the most ordinary state of the facts; for it is by the sale of his own finished article that each capitalist obtains the means of hiring labourers to renew the production; which is virtually the same thing as if, instead of selling the article for money and giving the money to his labourers, he gave the article itself to the labourers, and they sold it for their daily bread.

Assuming, therefore, that the labourer is paid in the very article he produces, it is evident that, when any saving of expense takes place in the production of that article, if the labourer still receives the same cost of production as before, he must receive an increased quantity, in the very same ratio in which the productive power of capital has been increased. But, if so, the outlay of the capitalist will bear exactly the same proportion to the return as it did before; and profits will not rise.

The variations, therefore, in the rate of profits, and those in the cost of production of wages, go hand in hand, and are inseparable. Mr. Ricardo's principle, that profits cannot rise unless wages fall, is strictly true, if by low wages be meant not merely wages which are the produce of a smaller quantity of labour, but wages which are produced at less cost, reckoning labour and previous profits together. But the interpretation which some economists have put upon Mr. Ricardo's doctrine, when they explain it to mean that profits depend upon the proportion which the labourers collectively receive of the aggregate produce, will not hold at all; for that, in our first example, remained the same, and yet profits rose.

The only expression of the law of profits, which seems to be correct, is, that they depend upon the cost of production of wages. This must be received as the ultimate principle.

From this may be deduced all the corollaries which Mr. Ricardo and others have drawn from his theory of profits as expounded by himself. The cost of production of the wages of one labourer for a year, is the result of two concurrent elements or factors, viz., First, the quantity of commodities which the state of the labour market affords to him; Secondly, the cost of production of each of those commodities. It follows, that the rate of profits can never rise but in conjunction with one or other of two changes; First, a diminished remuneration of the labourer; or, Secondly, an improvement in production, or an extension of commerce, by which any of the articles habitually consumed by the labourer may be obtained at smaller cost. (If the improvement be in any article which is not consumed by the labourer, it merely lowers the price of that article, and thereby benefits capitalists and all other people so far as they are consumers of that particular article, and may be said to increase gross profit, but not the rate of profit.)

So, on the other hand, the rate of profit cannot fall, unless concurrently with one of two events: First, an improvement in the labourer's condition; or, Secondly, an increased difficulty of producing or importing some article which the labourer habitually consumes. The progress of population and cultivation has a tendency to lower profits through the latter of these two channels, owing to the well known law of the application of capital to land, that a double capital does not *ceteris paribus* yield a double produce. There is, therefore, a tendency in the rate of profits to fall with the progress of society. But there is also an antagonist tendency of profits to rise, by the successive introduction of improvements in agriculture, and in the production of those manufactured articles which the labourers consume. Supposing, therefore, that the actual comforts of the labourer remain the same, profits will fall or rise, according as population, or improvements in the production of food and other necessaries, advance fastest.

The rate of profits, therefore, tends to *fall* from the following causes: First, an increase of capital beyond population, producing increased competition for labour; Secondly, an increase of population, occasioning a demand for an increased quantity of food, which must be produced at a greater cost. The rate of profits tends to rise from the following causes: First, an increase of population beyond capital, producing increased competition for employment; Secondly, improvements producing increased cheapness of necessaries, and other articles habitually consumed by the labourer.

The circumstances which regulate the rate of interest have usually been treated, even by professed writers on political economy, in a vague, loose, and unscientific manner. It has, however, been felt that there is some connection between the rate of interest and the rate of profit; that (to use the words of Adam Smith) much will be given for money, when much can be made of it. It has been felt, also, that the fluctuations in the market rate of interest froze day to day, are determined, like other matters of bargain and sale, by demand and supply. It has, therefore, been considered as an established principle, that the rate of interest varies from day to day according to the quantity of capital offered or called for on loan; but conforms on the average of years to a standard determined by the rate of profits, and bearing some proportion to that rate—but a proportion which few attempts have been made to define.

In consequence of these views, it has been customary to judge of the general rate of profits at any time or place, by the rate of interest at that time and place: It being supposed that the rate of interest, though liable to temporary fluctuations, can never vary for any long period of time unless profits vary; a notion which appears to us to be erroneous.

It was observed by Adam Smith, that profits may be considered as divided into two parts, of which one may properly be considered as the remuneration for the use of the capital itself, the other as the reward of the labour of superintending its employment; and that the former of these will correspond with the rate of interest. The producer who borrows capital to employ it in his business, will consent to pay, for the use of it, all that remains of the profits he can make by it, after reserving what he considers reasonable remuneration for the trouble and risk which he incurs by borrowing and employing it.

This remark is just; but it seems necessary to give greater precision to the ideas which it involves.

The difference between the profit which can be made by the use of capital, and the interest which will be paid for it, is rightly characterized as wages of superintendence. But to infer from this that it is regulated by entirely the same principles as other wages, would be to push the analogy too far. It is wages, but wages paid by a commission upon the capital employed. If the general rate of profit is ten per cent, and the rate of interest five per cent, the wages of superintendence will be five per cent; and though one borrower employ a capital of 100,000l., another no more than 100l., the labour of both will be rewarded with the same per cent, though, in the one case, this symbol will represent an income of 5l., in the other case, of 5,000l. Yet it cannot be pretended that the labour of the two borrowers differs in this proportion. The rule, therefore, that equal quantities of labour of equal hardness and skill are equally remunerated, does not hold of this kind of labour. The wages of any other labour are here an inapplicable criterion.

The wages of superintendence are distinguished from ordinary wages by another peculiarity, that they are not paid in advance out of capital, like the wages of all other labourers, but merge in the profit, and are not realized until the production is completed. This takes them entirely out of the ordinary law of wages. The wages of labourers who are paid in advance, are regulated by the number of competitors compared with the amount of capital; the labourers can consume no more than what has been previously accumulated. But there is no such limit to the remuneration of a kind of labour which is not paid for out of wealth previously accumulated, but out of that produce which it is itself employed in calling into existence.

When these circumstances are duly weighed, it will be perceived, that although profit may be correctly analyzed into interest and wages of superintendence, we ought not to lay it down as the law of interest, that it is profits *minus* the wages of superintendence. Of the two expressions, it would be decidedly the more correct, that the wages of superintendence are regulated by the rate of interest, or are equal to profits minus interest. In strict propriety, neither expression would be allowable. Interest, and the wages of superintendence, can scarcely be said to depend upon one another. They are to one another in the same relation as wages and profits are. They are like two buckets in a well; when one rises, the other descends, but neither of the two motions is the cause of the other; both are simultaneous effects of the same cause, the turning of the windlass.

There are among the capitalists of every country a considerable number who are habitually, and almost necessarily, lenders; to whom scarcely any difference between what they could receive for their money and what could be made by it, would be an equivalent for incurring the risk and labour of carrying on business. In this predicament is the property of widows and orphans; of many public bodies; of charitable institutions; most property which is vested in trustees; and the property of a great number of persons unused to business, and who have a distaste for it, or whose other occupations prevent their engaging in it. How large a proportion of the property lent to the nation comes under this description, has been pointed out in Mr. Tooke's *Considerations on the State of the Currency.*

There is another large class, consisting of bankers, bill brokers, and others, who are money lenders by profession; who enter into that profession with the intention of making such gains as it will yield them, and who would not be induced to change their business by any but a very strong pecuniary inducement.

There is, therefore, a large class of persons who are habitually lenders. On the other hand, all persons in business may be considered as habitually borrowers. Except in times of stagnation, they are all desirous of extending their business beyond their own capital, and are never desirous of lending any portion of their capital except for very short periods, during which they cannot advantageously invest it in their own trade.

There is, in short, a productive class, and there is, besides, a class technically styled the monied class, who live upon the interest of their capital, without engaging personally in the work of production.

The class of borrowers may be considered as unlimited. There is no quantity of capital that could be offered to be lent, which the productive classes would not be willing to borrow, at any rate of interest which would afford them the slightest excess of profit above a bare equivalent for the additional risk, incurred by that transaction, of the evils attendant on insolvency. The only assignable limit to the inclination to borrow, is the power of giving security: The producers would find it difficult to borrow more than an amount equal to their own capital. If more than half the capital of the country were in the hands of persons who preferred lending it to engaging personally in business, and if the surplus were greater than could be invested in loans to government, or in mortgages upon the property of unproductive consumers; the competition of lenders would force down the rate of interest very low. A certain portion of the monied class would be obliged either to sacrifice their predilections by engaging in business, or to lend on inferior security; and they would accordingly accept, where they could obtain good security, an abatement of interest equivalent to the difference of risk.

This is an extreme case. Let us put an extreme case of a contrary kind. Suppose that the wealthy people of any country, not relishing in idle life, and having a strong taste for gainful labour, were generally indisposed to accept of a smaller income in order to be relieved from the labour and anxiety of business. Every producer in flourishing circumstances would be eager to borrow, and few willing to lend. Under these circumstances the rate of interest would differ very little from the rate of profit. The trouble of managing a business is not proportionally increased by an increase of the magnitude of the business; and a very small surplus profit above the rate of interest, would therefore be a sufficient inducement to capitalists to borrow.

We may even conceive a people whose habits were such, that in order to induce them to lend, it might be necessary to offer them a rate of interest fully equal to the ordinary rate of profit. In that case, of course, the productive classes would scarcely ever borrow. But government, and the unproductive classes, who do not borrow in order to make a profit by the loan, but from the pressure of a real or supposed necessity, might still be ready to borrow at this high rate.

Although the inclination to borrow has no *fixed* or *necessary* limit except the power of giving security, yet it always, in point of fact, stops short of this; from the uncertainty of the prospects of any individual producer, which generally indisposes him to involve himself to the full extent of his means of payment. There is never any permanent want of market for things in general; but there may be so for the commodity which any one individual is producing; and even if there is a demand for the commodity, people may not buy it of him but of some other. There are, consequently, never more than a portion of the producers, the state of whose business encourages them to add to their capital by borrowing; and even these are disposed to borrow only as much as they see an *immediate* prospect of profitably employing. There is, therefore, a practical limit to the demands of borrowers at any given instant; and when these demands are all satisfied, any additional capital offered on loan can find an investment only by a reduction of the rate of interest.

The amount of borrowers being given (and by the amount of borrowers is here meant the aggregate sum which people are willing to borrow at some given rate), the rate of interest will depend upon the quantity of capital owned by people who are unwilling or unable to engage in trade. The circumstances which determine this, are, on the one hand, the degree in which a taste for business, or an aversion to it, happens to be prevalent among the classes possessed of property; and on the other hand, the amount of the annual accumulation from the earnings of labour. Those who accumulate from their wages, fees, or salaries, have, of course, (speaking generally) no means of investing their savings except by lending them to others; their occupations prevent them from personally superintending any employment.

Upon these circumstances, then, the rate of interest depends upon the amount of borrowers being given. And the counter-proposition equally holds, that, the above circumstances being given, the rate of interest depends upon the amount of borrowers.

Suppose, for example, that when the rate of interest has adjusted itself to the existing state of the circumstances which affect the disposition to borrow and to lend, a war breaks out, which induces government, for a series of years, to borrow annually a large sum of money. During the whole of this period, the rate of interest will remain considerably above what it was before, and what it will be afterward.

Before the commencement of the supposed war, all persons who were disposed to lend at the then rate of interest, had found borrowers, and their capital was invested. This may be assumed; for if any capital had been seeking for a borrower at the existing rate of interest, and unable to find one, its owner would have offered it at a rate slightly below the existing rate. He would, for instance, have bought into the funds, at a slight advance of price; and thus set at liberty the capital of some fundholder, who, the funds yielding a lower interest, would have been obliged to accept a lower interest from individuals.

Since, then, all who were willing to lend their capital at the market rate, have already lent it, government will not be able to borrow unless by offering higher interest. Though, with the existing habits of the possessors of disposable capital, an increased number cannot be found who are willing to lend at the existing rate, there are doubtless some who will be induced to lend by the temptation of a higher rate. The same temptation will also induce some persons to invest, in the purchase of the new stock, what they would otherwise have expended unproductively in increasing their establishments, or productively, in improving their estates. The rate of interest will rise just sufficiently to call forth an increase of lenders to the amount required.

This, we apprehend, to be the cause why the rate of interest in this country was so high, as it is well known to have been, during the last war. It is, therefore, by no means to be inferred, as some have done, that the general rate of profits was unusually high during the same period, because interest was so. Supposing the rate of profits to have been precisely the same during the war, as before or after it, the rate of interest would nevertheless have risen, from the causes and in the manner above described.

The practical use of the preceding investigation is, to moderate the confidence with which inferences are frequently drawn with respect to the rate of profit from evidence regarding the rate of interest; and to show that although the rate of profit is one of the elements which combine to determine the rate of interest, the latter is also acted upon by causes peculiar to itself, and may either rise or fall, both temporarily and permanently, while the general rate of profits remains unchanged.

The introduction of banks, which perform the function of lenders and loan brokers, with or without that of issuers of paper money, produces some further anomalies in the rate of interest, which, have not, so far as we are aware, been hitherto brought within the pale of exact science.

If bankers were merely a class of middlemen between the lender and the borrower; if they merely received deposits of capital from those who had it lying unemployed in their hands, and lent this, together with their own capital, to the productive classes, receiving interest for it, and paying interest in their turn to those who had placed capital in their hands; the effect of the operations of banking on the rate of interest would be to lower it in some slight degree. The banker receives and collects together sums of money much too small, when taken individually, to render it worthwhile for the owners to look out for an investment, but which in the aggregate form a considerable amount. This amount may be considered a clear addition to the productive capital of the country; at least, to the capital in activity at any moment. And as this addition to the capital accrues wholly to that part of it which is not employed by the owners, but lent to other producers, the natural effect is a diminution of the rate of interest.

The banker, to the extent of his own private capital (the expenses of his business being first paid), is a lender at interest. But, being subject to risk and trouble fully equal to that which belongs to most other employments, he cannot be satisfied with the mere interest even of his whole capital: He must have the ordinary profits of stock, or he will not engage in the business. The state of banking must be such as to hold out to him the prospect of adding to the interest of what remains of his own capital after paying the expenses of his business, interest upon capital deposited with him, in sufficient amount to make up, after paying the expenses, the ordinary profit which could be derived from his own capital in any productive employment. This will be accomplished in one of two ways.

1. If the circumstances of society are such as to furnish a ready investment of disposable capital; (as for instance in London, where the public funds and other securities, of undoubted stability, and affording great advantages for receiving the interest without trouble and realizing the principal without difficulty when required, tempt all persons who have sums of importance lying idle, to invest them on their own account without the intervention of any middleman) the deposits with bankers consist chiefly of small sums likely to be wanted in a very short period for current expenses, and the interest on which would seldom be worth the trouble of calculating it. Bankers, therefore, do not allow any interest on their deposits. After paying the expenses of their business, all the rest of the interest they receive is clear gain. But as the circumstances of banking, as of all other modes of employing capital, will on the average be such as to afford to a person entering into the business a prospect of realizing the ordinary, and no more than the ordinary, profits upon his own capital; the gains of each banker by the investment of his deposits, will not on the average exceed what is necessary to make up his gains on his own capital to the ordinary rate. It is, of course, competition, which brings about this limitation. Whether competition operates by lowering the rate of interest, or by dividing the business among a larger number, it is difficult to decide. Probably it operates in both ways; but it is by no means impossible that it may operate in the latter way alone: Just as an increase in the number of physicians does not lower the fees, though it diminishes an average competitor's chance of obtaining them.

It is not impossible that the disposition of the lenders might be such, that they would cease to lend rather than acquiesce in any reduction of the rate of interest. If so, the arrival of a new lender, in the person of a banker of deposit, would not lower the rate of interest in any considerable degree. A slight fall would take place, and with that exception things would be as before, except that the capital in the hands of the banker would have put itself into the place of an equal portion of capital belonging to other lenders, who would themselves have engaged in business (e.g., by subscribing to some joint-stock company, or entering into commandite). Bankers' profits would then be limited to the ordinary rate chiefly by the division of the business among many banks, so that each on the average would receive no more interest on his deposits than would suffice to make up the interest on his own capital to the ordinary rate of profit after paying all expenses.

2. But if the circumstances of society render it difficult and inconvenient for persons who wish to live upon the interest of their money, to seek an investment for themselves, the bankers become agents for this specific purpose: Large as well as small sums are deposited with them, and they allow interest to their customers. Such is the practice of the Scotch banks, and of most of the country banks in England. Their customers, not living at any of the great seats of money transactions, prefer entrusting their capital to somebody on the spot, whom they know, and in whom they confide. He invests their money on the best terms he can, and pays to them such interest as he can afford to give; retaining a compensation for his own risk and trouble. This compensation is fixed by the competition of the market. The rate of interest is no further lowered by this operation, than inasmuch as it brings together the lender and the borrower in a safe and expeditious manner. The lender incurs less risk, and a larger proportion, therefore, of the holders of capital are willing to be lenders.

When a banker, in addition to his other functions, is also an issuer of paper money, he gains an advantage similar to that which the London bankers derive from their deposits. To the extent to which he can put forth his notes, he has so much the more to lend, without himself having to pay any interest for it.

If the paper is convertible, it cannot get into circulation permanently without displacing specie, which goes abroad and brings back an equivalent value. To the extent of this value, there is an increase of the capital of the country; and the increase accrues solely to that part of the capital which is employed in loans.

If the paper is inconvertible, and instead of displacing specie depreciates the currency, the banker, by issuing it, levies a tax on every person who has money in his hands or due to him. He thus appropriates to himself a portion of the capital of other people, and a portion of their revenue. The capital might have been intended to be lent, or it might have been intended to be employed by the owner; such part of it as was intended to be employed by the owner now changes its destination, and is lent. The revenue was either intended to be accumulated, in which case it had already become capital, or it was intended to be spent: In this last case, revenue is converted into capital, and thus, strange as it may appear, the depreciation of the currency, when effected in this way, operates to a certain extent as a forced accumulation. This, indeed, is no palliation of its iniquity. Though A might have spent his property unproductively, B ought not to be permitted to rob him of it because B will expend it on productive labour.

In any supposable case, however, the issue of paper money by bankers increases the proportion of the whole capital of the country which is destined to be lent. The rate of interest must therefore fall, until some of the lenders give over lending, or until the increase of borrowers absorbs the whole.

But a fall of the rate of interest, sufficient to enable the money market to absorb the whole of the paper loans, may not be sufficient to reduce the profits of a lender who lends what costs him nothing, to the ordinary rate of profit upon his capital. Here, therefore, competition will operate chiefly by dividing the business. The notes of each bank will be confined within so narrow a district, or will divide the supply of a district with so many other banks, that on the average each will receive no larger amount of interest on his notes than will make up the interest on his own capital to the ordinary rate of profit.

Even in this way, however, the competition has the effect, to a certain limited extent, of lowering the rate of interest; for the power of bankers to receive interest on more than their capital attracts a greater amount of capital into the banking business than would otherwise flow into it; and this greater capital being all lent, interest will fall in consequence.

Notes

1. It would be easy to go over in the same manner any other case. For instance, we may suppose, that, instead of dispensing with the whole of the fixed capital, material, etc., and taking on labourers in equal number to those by whom these were produced, half only of the fixed capital and material is dispensed with; so that, instead of sixty labourers and a fixed capital worth sixty quarters of corn, we have eighty labourers and a fixed capital worth thirty. The numerical statement of this case is more intricate than that in the text, but the result is not different.

ABOUT THE PUBLISHER

Coventry House Publishing is a traditional publisher of adult fiction and non-fiction titles. Founded in Dublin, Ohio in 2012, we're beginning a long tradition of serving readers and authors across the country, one book at a time.

We pride ourselves on the quality, meaningful work we publish. Our primary genres of focus include business & economics, sports & recreation, education & social science, and fiction & entertainment. Please visit our website, www.coventrybooks.com, for more information about our featured books and authors.

CPSIA information can be obtained
at www.ICGtesting.com
Printed in the USA
LVHW080023050821
694587LV00021B/946